A SHADOW AND A SONG

A SHADOW AND A SONG

The Struggle to Save an Endangered Species

Mark Jerome Walters

CHELSEA GREEN PUBLISHING COMPANY
Post Mills, Vermont

Title page illustration by Joan Waltermire.
A Shadow and a Song was designed and formatted by
Kate Mueller/Electric Dragon Productions.
It was printed at Maple-Vail Press on recycled paper.

Library of Congress Cataloging-in-Publication Data

Walter, Mark Jerome
A shadow and a song: the struggle to save an endangered species /
Mark Walters.
p. cm.
Includes bibiliographical references and index.
ISBN 0-930031-58-X (cloth: alk. paper): $21.95
1. Dusky seaside sparrow—Florida. 2. Extinct birds—Florida. I. Title.
QL696.P2438W35 1992   92-16333
598'.042—dc20   CIP

For you, Brianna

And in memory of your mother, Toi Walters Charlton

And Andy Charlton

What are the roots that clutch, what branches grow
out of this stony rubbish? Son of man,
You cannot say, or guess, for you know only
A heap of broken images, where the sun beats
And the dead tree gives no shelter, the cricket no relief,
And the dry stone no sound of water.

T. S. Eliot

Acknowledgments

"The essential matter of history is not what happened but what people thought or said about it," Frederic Maitland wrote. Although this book is also about *what* happened, those who shared their thoughts and feelings are much a part of the history.

My gratitude to Gail Baker, Kenneth E. Black, Joseph D. Carroll, Dwight Cooley, Lisa Danforth, Jim Ellis, Lon Ellis, Pete Gallagher, Bill Gillett, John W. Hardy, F. Eugene Hester, Bill Leenhouts, Joy Mitchell, Keven Myers, William Post, Lisanne Renner, Paul W. Sykes, Jr., D. Scott Taylor, Charles Trost, Lovett Williams, Jr., Lee Wenner, Dorn Whitman, Dick Young, and the late Johnny Johnson. All of them provided important information for this book.

I am especially indebted to Charlie Cook, Herb Kale, Jack Salmela, Brian Sharp, and Chuck Trost for their generosity of time and patience during long personal interviews and numerous telephone conversations. Kale and Sharp reviewed not only parts of the first draft, but read entire subsequent manuscripts for errors, omissions, and inconsistencies. Cook, Salmela, and Trost also reviewed relevant parts of the manuscript.

Ian and Margo Baldwin and the staff at Chelsea Green nurtured this book, but they never pushed—granting me a luxury of time and understanding for which I am grateful. Joni Praded, my editor and friend, offered constructive criticism throughout the various drafts. Cannon Labrie edited the final manuscript. Helen Whybrow provided valuable assistance throughout the writing and production of the book.

The International Program at Tufts University School of Veterinary Medicine has been my home away from home for the last four years, and the people there have been my family, especially Dr. Albert Sollod, Dr. Chip Stem, and Sheila Moffat. And I shall always owe a depth of gratitude to George Archibald of the International Crane Foundation, who encouraged my writing about endangered species.

My mother Antoinette has supported me always in my endeavors, and but for the many books she gave me as a child, I might never have written one as an adult. I wish to thank my family in Hawaii, especially Helen Tomasu and Kiki Tomasu, for their prayers each daybreak, and the late Tom Tomasu.

To more than anyone else, I am indebted to Mariko Sakurai for her patience and generosity.

Contents

Prologue

On the morning of July 16, 1969—I was in high school—I stood with my parents, brothers, sisters, aunts, and uncles on Merritt Island, Florida, about five miles from the Kennedy Space Center and peered across the Banana River as *Apollo 11* lifted off for the moon. Amethyst starlets of wild verbena grew along the byway. A few lean palms, bent westward by prevailing winds, stood near the water; a grove of Australian pines, long tassels dropping, hunched behind us. We were a cluster of modern well-wishers gathered on the shore of a river that might have flowed straight from the Pleistocene. The voice of Mission Control, blaring over car radios, counted down the seconds. At ignition, a puff of smoke rose beyond a low line of mangroves across the river. Several seconds passed before the rumbling reached us. A gigantic cloud of dark billowing smoke enveloped the launchpad, and the rocket gradually rose through it. It accelerated upward and pitched eastward, receding above the Atlantic and leaving a massive contrail reflected in the river. The rocket must have remained in view for four or five minutes, and as we stood there, gazing at the distant structures of Kennedy Space Center rising beyond the green horizon, each of us sensed the historical importance of the event. Some people wept aloud. Walter Cronkite's voice, unsteady and emotional, gushed over the radio. I snapped two pictures of the launch with a Polaroid camera, photographs that stand today in silver frames on my bookshelf—reminders of the many changes reaching backward and forward from an event that transformed the environs of Merritt Island from a rural earthly outpost into what seemed like a gateway to the universe.

There was a time when the name Florida evoked in many people's minds vistas of the last remaining subtropical wilderness in America: vast wetlands, thousands of miles of scalloped white coastline, and open skies with flocks of roseate spoonbills descending to roost. In the minds of many, Florida was America's Garden of Eden. Even today the state has more than 475 species of birds (the largest number of indigenous avian species in the continental United States); more than 3000 native plant species; at least 140 native species of reptiles and amphibians (40 kinds of frogs and toads alone); and 94 species of wild mammals. Since William Bartram visited Florida more than two hundred years ago, an expedition through the state was a rite of passage for almost all the great American naturalists. With the coming of the space age, the land's fabulous natural history became overshadowed by its promising technological future. The state's image as wilderness was suddenly transformed into one at the cutting edge of technology. The once sleepy town of Titusville, swelling with people and pride, took the name Miracle City. This small, friendly riverine outpost was suddenly hooked on the stars.

The journey to the moon was the strangest of expeditions, for when the explorers reached their destination they made no territorial claims, nor hoped to return with appreciable wealth. The astronauts traveled to a land known to be far poorer than the place they had left behind—going from a planet of airy-winged birds and shimmering rivers to a waterless, airless, dusty, lifeless, pockmarked orb. It was for all practical purposes a journey from somewhere to nowhere. As the module perched silently on the moon's carpet, astronaut Buzz Aldrin stood before the abort guidance computer, pulled out a wafer, a small chalice, and wine, and celebrated a Eucharistic ritual two thousand years old. Radio listeners on Earth were enthralled as Aldrin looked through the window of the landing craft over the Sea of Tranquility and radioed of the "magnificent desolation" surrounding him. Upon the astronauts' return, President Richard Nixon proclaimed the time the "greatest week in the history of the world since creation."

I had seen rocket launches before, for I had grown up in Brevard County, Florida. For a time our family lived in a small beach house that sat on a dune crowned in a tangle of sea grape, twenty miles south of Merritt Island. A row of shaggy Australian pines stood behind the house, and twenty yards beyond, a lonely bar known as the Merrimac—two motley structures along an otherwise mostly deserted stretch of beach. Sometimes at night I wandered over to sit on the lowest of the three cement steps at the front of the bar, gazing up the darkened beach and wondering about rockets, while music softly drifted through the slatted windows on the rich and intoxicating aroma of burning tobacco, and my father sat inside drinking beer. Once I stood knee-deep in the surf off the beach as a Redstone rocket lifted off with a flash far to the north.

In the 1950s, before the building of the Kennedy Space Center, launches originated from Cape Canaveral Air Force

Station, a facility that covered part of the peninsula. A few technicians would drive along the old narrow road out to the Cape, construct a small derricklike gantry on a poured cement footing, hoist an empty rocket fuselage upright, fuel it as one fills an automobile at a self-service station, then ignite it. If it went up, that was great; if it blew up, they would come back another day and try again. In those days rocket launches lacked the potential for large enough disaster for the world to be interested. By the late 1960s the mission involved more than twenty thousand technicians and was carried on live television around the world.

The lunar flight spawned grandiose schemes of self-contained space colonies in gigantic cylinders that would rotate to simulate gravity. Arguments erupted within the scientific community as to how fast these structures should turn. Prominent features in the graphic renditions of the space colonies were palm trees, luxuriant foliage, and great open places with serpentine rivers meandering through rolling landscape, while slender-winged birds glided overhead. In short, the envisioned colonies would contain the most of what we feared we could least do without—the forests, the animals, and the rivers that spoke to an awareness older than ourselves.

The flight of Apollo brought sweeping changes to the once wild environs of the Banana and Indian Rivers. Byways became highways, and just about any land that could turn a profit was put up for sale.

With most far-reaching industrial undertakings, as with Apollo, the profoundest ecological changes are rarely foreseen. Of those that are, the worst among them are usually ignored.

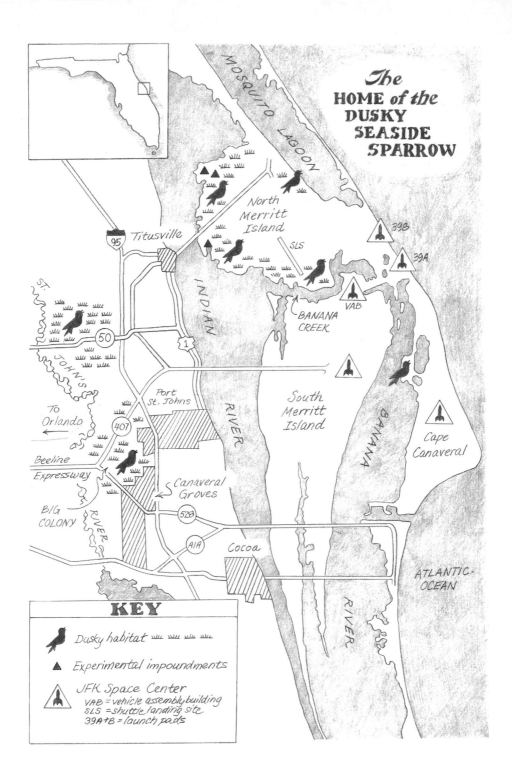

The
HOME of the
DUSKY
SEASIDE
SPARROW

MOSQUITO LAGOON

Titusville

North
Merritt
Island

SLS

39B

39A

VAB

BANANA
CREEK

95

ST. JOHN'S

50

1

INDIAN RIVER

South
Merritt
Island

BANANA RIVER

Cape
Canaveral

Port
St. Johns

To
Orlando

407

Beeline
Expressway

BIG
COLONY

RIVER

Canaveral
Groves

528

A1A

Cocoa

ATLANTIC
OCEAN

RIVER

KEY

Dusky habitat

Experimental impoundments

JFK Space Center
VAB = vehicle assembly building
SLS = shuttle landing site
39A+B = launch pads

1

An Island
Between Two Rivers

Envision the narrow spit of fine, bone-colored sand known as the Canaveral Peninsula stretching north and south a hundred miles along the east Florida coast. An almost unbroken chain of dunes runs along the peninsula like the bleached spine of an ancient beast. Above the unencumbered beaches, pelicans glide like pterodactyls. Tracks of giant loggerhead sea turtles amble toward the embankment of dunes. This long narrow peninsula is bordered on the east by the Atlantic Ocean, and on the west by a wide torpid river whose shallows fan into a vast marsh that fades with the western horizon. Leeward breezes carry the fragrance of swamp rose across the marsh. In the river lies Merritt Island—a two-part island—separated by a watery slough known as Banana Creek. North Merritt, about ten miles long and eight or nine miles wide, is slightly smaller than the longer and narrower South Merritt. Headwatered in the shallows of Mosquito Lagoon to the north, the river forks as it reaches the island. The branch along the eastern side is the Banana River; along the western, the Indian River. Envision all this, and you have seen a land that once belonged to the dusky seaside sparrow.

The dusky seaside sparrow was never widespread. Even at the peak of its population, the sparrow had among the most limited distribution of any bird in North America, confined to a portion of a single county in Florida. Two small, separate groups comprised the entire known distribution. A few thousand birds may have once lived on Merritt Island. Several thousand more lived inland about ten miles to the west, along the peaceful St. Johns River. These two locales, both in Brevard County and within twelve miles of Titusville, were the known historical sum of the sparrow's tenuous existence. Although sufficient to sustain the bird through ten thousand years of prosperity, the delicate hold proved too fragile for modern encroachment.

While millions of species have thrived before slowly being drawn on a course toward extinction, the dusky seaside sparrow was different. It was not an unfit contender in the "Darwinian" struggle for existence. For thousands of years the sparrow competed successfully, only to have its habitat willfully destroyed within a period of twenty-five years. The sparrow's recent history, therefore, was anything but natural. And its death did not just happen; it was caused.

The dusky's tragedy is singular in that nothing was achieved through its extinction that could not have been gained through its survival—neither the diking of the marshes, which heavily contributed to the sparrow's demise, nor the resultant mosquito control, on which timely success of the moon mission partly depended.

Because of resident hordes of mosquitoes, the dusky's habitat across North Merritt Island resisted human settlement until the 1960s. South Merritt Island, dryer and more welcoming than North Merritt, had been quilted into neat rows of citrus groves by the early 1900s. Growers found the well-drained sand-and-marl soil ideal for growing oranges and grapefruits. Warm air from the Gulf Stream wafted inland on easterly sea breezes, loosening the grip of would-be freezes.

In the 1930s my father, Linwood Walters, about nineteen at the time, ran a gas station on South Merritt. Later, when he married, he and my mother moved into a house owned by my maternal grandfather, behind a shaggy grove of Australian pines on the west bank of the Indian River in the little town of Eau Gallie, a few miles south of Merritt Island, and not far from dusky country. One Christmas Day the house burned. We moved, for a time, to the small house on the beach.

Before the house at Sunny Point burned, my grandfather used to take leisurely excursions up the Indian in his mahogany yacht, *Sunshine III*, past the confluence with the Banana, along the house-dotted shores of South Merritt, past the wild marshy fringes of North Merritt, threading his way through vistas of swaying grass toward Mosquito Lagoon. Lifting his ancient heavy binoculars to his eyes, on a good day he might see deer, bobcat, bear, turkeys, bald eagles, panthers, and many other animals. Today this same route along the Indian comprises a busy link in the Intracoastal Waterway, and there is scarcely a mammal, save for humans, to be seen. Where my grandfather passed beneath two wooden bridges as he motored to the lagoon, today the same journey would take one beneath seven spans. Although I was not yet around to accompany him on these trips, the sojourns became material for his tales in later years, many of which he related to me from his hospital bed, where he died of emphysema in 1964. It was there that I first heard of a rare and mysterious sparrow on Merritt Island. My grandfather never gave it a name but promised to take me there to see it for myself one day—just as soon as he recovered. The promise was not taken lightly by a ten-year-old. My grandfather did not live long enough to fulfill it. Nor could he have imagined that the bird he spoke of would outlive him by less than twenty-five years.

Years later, with most of my family having moved from Florida, I would return to write about the dusky seaside sparrow. Over several years and more than a dozen trips, I gathered correspondence and visited many of the people involved with the bird. Naturally, these sojourns to Brevard County also became expeditions in search of the places where I grew up, for those same forces that destroyed the sparrow ultimately rendered unrecognizable nearly every place I had known as a child.

Merritt Island adjoins the bony knuckle of Cape Canaveral, the easternmost reach of the peninsula, by a panorama of swales. The dusky's quiet presence along the Canaveral Peninsula was overshadowed by the land's human history. Visible from miles at sea, the Cape was first charted by Spanish explorer Ponce de Leon in 1513 and named, during an expedition seven years later, by slave trader Francisco Gordillo, who put ashore in small boats and fought a fierce battle with the indigenous people. Gordillo's men wore chain-mail armor, and the warriors' arrows splintered as they struck it, sending penetrating slivers between the links, killing and wounding many of Gordillo's men. The fire-hardened shafts had been made from stiff, canelike reeds collected from a large marsh at the southern bight of the Cape. Barely escaping with his life, Gordillo called the place Canaveral, or "canebearer." The name remained for almost five hundred years, making it among the oldest place names on the Atlantic coast of North America. In 1963, after the assassination of John F. Kennedy, Lyndon Johnson insisted on renaming it Cape Kennedy. Not until Johnson's death ten years later was the Cape's rightful name was restored. Today only the space center proper, which occupies part of Merritt Island and a portion of the Cape, retains Kennedy's name.

The Canaveral Peninsula was noted for its rainbows, birds, and spectacular sunsets. As described by the Federal Writers' Project, the "western sky flushes rose behind the dark screen of Australian pines above the beach as the eastern heavens merge with a cobalt sea. A rainbow fragment is perhaps reflected momentarily in jade-green water; under the darkening sky the tumbling surf grows wine-dark, and a final touch of color is often added as a line of tropical birds rises, low and far away, and drops from view." The Cape, like Merritt Island proper, was also a garden for botanists. In the early 1900s naturalist C. T. Simpson identified forty-three tropical and twenty-five warm temperate varieties of tree on the Cape, including ironwood, gumbo limbo, soapberry, torchwood, strangling fig, paradise tree, pond apple, and necklace bean.

The Canaveral Peninsula, which forms a protective barrier between the Atlantic and low-lying Merritt Island, is in large part responsible for the island's existence—and so, too, for the dusky seaside sparrow's. So complete was the protective barrier between the ocean and the rivers that the Merritt Island salt marsh existed largely independent of the lunar tides. Rather, the island's tides were driven by rain and prevailing winds that sometimes drove the river into the marsh. Only during the highest spring and fall tides could the ocean push into distant reaches of the river. In fact, parts of the North Merritt Island marsh were dry for almost ten months of the year. Other parts frequently, although unpredictably, flooded.

Of the thousands of kinds of plants in North America, a select few thrive in the salt marsh—among them, a group of grasses belonging to the genus *Spartina*, a name originating from the Greek word for a cord once made from the tough leaves of a Mediterranean species. The dense, low *Spartina patens* dominates the marshes of northern latitudes; the taller, coarser *S. alterniflora* dominates the southern. On Merritt Island as in the nearby St. Johns marshes, a third species, *S. bakeri* ruled. It grew about waist-high and could tolerate flooding only about seventy days a year, in contrast to *Spartina alterniflora*, which can survive in marshes inundated three hundred days a year. Each of the half-dozen species of *Spartina* has specialized to live with the cycles of a particular salt marsh.

Few plants in the Merritt Island marsh were more dependent on the comings and goings of the tide than was the *S. bakeri* that fringed the wide flats between the uplands and the riversides. The *Spartina*, also known as broomgrass (so named because it was once cut and bundled into brooms), provided shelter for the dusky, and it discouraged many of the bird's predators. In a sense, the marsh is inseparable from the broomgrass; by straining runoff between the thick bundles of roots, the plants trap silt that would otherwise be lost to the Indian and Banana Rivers and ultimately to the ocean. Collecting the sediment grain by grain, the *Spartina* slowly build a foundation of soil and peat that sustain many plants and animals. The plant-laden soil, in turn, acts as a buffer against storm surges.

Ranging up to two and a half miles wide, the vast expanses of broomgrass once fringed the river flats as far as the eye could see. On hot afternoons the marshes glistened like a sea of wheat. During hurricanes, sea winds roiled across the backbone of Cape Canaveral and blew through the tall stiff grass with a sound of woodwinds.

Spartina are, as a genus, marvelously adaptable. The Merritt Island marsh was a place of extremes—dry one day, wet the next, with dramatic shifts in temperature and salinity. The Spartina are able to live in salt water while keeping their internal juices fresh, despite drastic changes in the outside environment. Special root cells filter most of the salt out but allow fresh water to enter. The plants depend on the rain or tide to disperse the salt deposits left behind. When the plants transpire on hot days, any salt that managed to seep in is excreted through the leaves, forming tiny crystals that make the plants and the marsh sparkle in the sunlight. Rain or rising waters wash this away as well. While salt is omnipresent in the marsh, oxygen in the water-logged soil is scarce. Spartina have evolved tiny air sacs in their roots that store the oxygen for the plant's use in times of flooding. The air-pocketed roots leak oxygen into the surrounding soil, causing minute natural traces of iron in the ground to rust; this reddish brown ball of soil in turn becomes a microcosm for a community of oxygen-breathing microorganisms.

While broomgrass dominated the high marsh, in the lower marsh—but a few inches lower in elevation—grew dense low patches of salt hay, a short wiry plant of striking geometry, with long, slender, stiff leaves arranged in opposition along the stems. There were the bayoneted stalks of black needle rush, a coarse dark plant with tubular leaves ending in wickedly pointed tips. Lower in the marsh, the erect and translucent water-swollen jade-green stems of glasswort grew in thick mats. Lacking leaves, each stem ended in a spike; each of its minute flowers, nearly invisible without close inspection, was tucked into a separate tiny recess along the stem. Scarlet and yellow in late autumn, the glasswort offered one of the few dramatic seasonal color changes in the marsh. In the low marsh close to the river, thinning stands of broomgrass intermingled with the glasswort, creating a thick undercover into which duskies could escape from predators. So abundant was the production of plants in the marsh that through the seasons, the cycle of death and decay sent a steady supply of nutrient-rich detritus to the rivers' edges where minnows fed before abandoning the protective rivers for a life at sea. Higher in the marsh stood seaoxeye and tall groundsel-tree, and the firmer ground was criss-crossed by numerous creeks arranged like veins that emptied into small ponds, a few surrounded by the knobby-fingered roots of small mangroves. The pools were connected to the rivers by a labyrinth of meandering streams that ebbed and flowed with the water levels. Geographically speaking, Cape Canaveral and Merritt Island was a land of many languages— where ocean, beach, marsh, river, trade wind, and tide joined in endless negotiations for existence.

Toward the middle of Merritt Island was the "upland," which rose to a maximum of about fifteen feet. Historically these hot and crackling forests were covered by palmettos and slash pine and held an array of wildlife. By the 1950s hunters had eliminated many of the larger animals. The Florida panther, now verging on extinction, had more or less vanished from the island by 1950. The last black bear on Merritt Island was shot in 1951. The once abundant wild turkey is now a rare sight.

Merritt Island is still inhabited by some sixty-five kinds of amphibians and dozens of reptiles, including seven species of turtles. Rare sea turtles, including the Kemps Ridley, Atlantic green, Atlantic hawksbill, Atlantic leatherback, and Atlantic loggerhead, are found in the nearby lagoons. All but loggerheads face extinction. Sharing the waters off Merritt Island is the endangered manatee. Of all the large residents, today only the alligator is a common sight, having recovered from the mass slaughter earlier this century. Today fourteen federally listed endangered or threatened species of animals inhabit Merritt Island.

Worldwide, birds have suffered the most catastrophic toll. Of the some 8600 species recognized, more than 1000 are threatened with extinction, according to the International Council for Bird Preservation (ICBP). More than 500 species in North America are declining, including what were once among the commonest of birds. Starlings, invigorated by the expanding urban landscape, are among the few species that continue to increase.

Located along one of the main flyways for birds migrating between North and South America, in spring and fall Merritt Island historically hosted a diversity of species, including common and red-throated loons, horned and pied-billed grebes, brown and American-white pelicans, double-crested cormorants, glossy and white ibises, roseate spoonbills, geese, ducks, vultures, hawks, peregrine falcons, ospreys, the rare Everglades snail kite, quails, wild turkeys, limpkins, rails, gallinules, coots, some three dozen types of sandpipers, plovers, gulls, terns, and cuckoos. Few of these visitors bred in the Merritt Island marshes, but fed and rested there before continuing their long journeys. Offshore species such as gannets and five species of shearwaters, as well as Wilson's petrels, often visited the island.

Attesting to the resilience of nature in the face of man-made change, today Merritt Island is still regularly visited by some three hundred species of birds, including ten species of herons and egrets, and numerous species of geese and ducks. But the numbers of birds that once flourished on Merritt Island and along the so-called Mosquito Coast defies the imaginations of most birders today, for whom a modest squadron of wood storks descending to roost would seem the sight of a lifetime. In 1875 a Florida guide writer wrote of Merritt

Island, "Duck shooting is unsurpassed. In February and March the marshes along Mosquito Lagoon and Banana Creek are alive with these wildlife. I have seen millions of these within a space of a square mile. By one shot I have killed five different species—teal, mallard, gray widgeon, baldpates and the big, black English duck." Even as late as the 1950s, visitors spoke of having to cover their ears during thunderous takeoffs of thousands of ducks wildly thrashing their web feet against the water. Twenty-three species of duck still inhabit the island at one time of the year or another although their numbers today are in steep decline. Large flocks of warblers still descend on the island in spring and fall, and the groups of summering roseate spoonbills or the occasional red-pouched magnificent frigate birds may be seen.

Of the approximately eight hundred species of birds recognized in North America, only two evolved to live exclusively and permanently in the salt marsh—the clapper rails and the seaside sparrows. Of the more than half-dozen kinds of seaside sparrows currently recognized, only one highly specialized type had evolved over the millennia to thrive in the salt marshes of Brevard County: this was the dusky seaside sparrow.

2

The Sparrow

In the spring of 1954 Herbert William Kale II, an avid young birder from Trenton, New Jersey, rumbled over the wooden planks of the bridge between Titusville and Merritt Island in his brother's green 1949 Chevrolet, accompanied by several of his Theta Chi fraternity brothers from Rutgers University. Once over the Indian River, they drove across a causeway that entered the island between Puckett and Gator Creeks. When he stopped the car at the roadside and stepped out, Kale noticed almost immediately the raspy, three-note songs of darkly plumed sparrows. The birds seemed to be singing everywhere from the tops of the waist high broomgrass that fringed the island as far as Kale could see. At this time of the year the broomgrass was stiff and brown, with fresh spring growth sprouting from its bases. These were the first dusky seaside sparrows Kale had ever seen.

Kale's ostensible reason for this trip, taken during spring

break, was to spend a week on the beaches at Fort Lauderdale, but it soon dawned on the others that, as far as Kale was concerned, birding was all that mattered. The dusky was one of the prized species listed among the 750 others at that time in the *Checklist of North American Birds*, the bible of the dedicated bird watcher. Because of the bird's rarity, the dusky had a sizable following. Thousands of birders came annually from around the country to Merritt Island to see the rare sparrow.

Although similar in appearance to the other types of seaside sparrows, the darkly colored dusky was the most distinctive. The upper body feathers were rich brown to black, streaked with olive and gray. Its dark crown continued as a stripe down the back, over the rump and toward a sharply pointed tail. A dark brown patch surrounded each eye and, in addition to the narrow saffron eyebrows, a stroke of vibrant gamboge yellow highlighted the bend of each wing. Except for the pale highlighting on the end of the primary and secondary feathers, the wings shared the darkly colored markings of the back. The dusky's chin and throat were white, with narrow dark "whisker" marks running from the base of the bill to the throat. The boldly marked chest was the most distinctive feature, with black streaks or mottled patterns across a white breast. Below the chest the belly turned a soft white, which extended between the dusky's gray legs to the base of the tail. Chest thrown out in song, the dusky had a proud thrushlike presence—a standout among the usual drab browns and grays of the sparrow family.

Kale had come to the island at just the right time to see the male duskies vocally defending their territories. During the spring breeding season, the males were aggressive, advertising their territorial songs from the broomgrass. The females remained near their nests. Outside of breeding season, the males would have remained hidden in the grass, a strategy in keeping with the particular type of protection afforded by the marsh. As no trees or cover loomed overhead, flight was less effective than hiding as a way of escape. A predator would have a difficult time finding a sparrow in the grass.

In 1831 John James Audubon described the characteristic wariness of the seaside sparrows in general:

> The monotonous chirpings which one hears in almost every part of our maritime salt marshes, are produced by this bird . . . which may be seen at any hour of the day during the months of May and June, mounted on the tops of the rankest weeds which grow by the margins of the tide waters . . . whence it pours forth with much emphasis the few notes of which its song is composed. When one approaches it, it either seeks refuge amongst the grass, by descending along the stalks and blades of the weeds, or flies off to a short distance, with a continued flirting of its wings, then alights with a rapid descent and runs off with great nimbleness. . . . It is very difficult to shoot them unless when they are on the wing, as their movements while they run up and down the weeds are extremely rapid; but their flight is so direct and level, that a good marksman can easily kill them before they alight amongst the grass again. . . . Having one day shot a number of these birds, merely for the sake of practice, I had them made into a pie, which, however could not be eaten, on account of its fishy savour.

Kale watched enthralled as one male rose thirty or forty feet above its perch, burst into a musical flight song, then dropped back to the grass on quivering wings. Some of the sparrows emitted a rapid triple cadence *toodle-aeeee* while fluttering into the air, then descended to another perch where they emitted a decidedly less musical *chirp-chirp-chirp*. More mechanical than melodic, the song is sometimes transcribed in field guides as an anapestic *cut-aa-zheeeee*.

Donald J. Nicholson, a Florida egg collector who visited Merritt Island in 1926, had found the marshes "fairly sizzling with their peculiar songs." Nicholson wrote that the song "is preceded by two metallic notes in the same pitch resembling *Dick, Dick,* and followed by a buzzing which is hard to describe. Different males have different songs, and some have four or five different songs. Another phase of the song is a series of bubbling, zig-zag notes similar in character to the song of the marsh wrens."

The sparrow family is the product of more than 30 million years of evolution. Its most distant birdlike ancestor—as is apparently true of all birds—is *Archaeopteryx,* the feathered, poorly flying reptilian that emerged during the late Jurassic period about 150 million years ago. The earliest true sparrow fossils begin to appear in the Oligocene, 35 million years ago, during an epoch that also gave rise to cormorants, turkeys, pigeons, and parrots—each of which developed into a separate order. The sparrows belong to the order Passeriformes, or perching birds. This order is further subdivided into dozens of families. The sparrows, along with the warblers, tanagers, blackbirds, grosbeaks, and buntings, belong to the huge family Emberizidae. Stepping still further down the taxonomic stairway, the sparrows are subdivided into twenty or more genera, one of which is *Ammodramus.* Among its members are the Baird's, Henslow's, grasshopper, Le Conte's, sharp-tailed, and seaside sparrows. The seasides, which belong to the species *maritimus,* "shore dwellers," currently include more than a half-dozen subspecies. Among the most limited in distribution of the lot was the dusky seaside sparrow, *Ammodramus maritimus nigrescens,* its subspecies name meaning "becoming black." One could spend a lifetime mastering this taxonomy and know almost nothing about the dusky.

The vagaries of classification are usually of little more than academic interest. But the dusky's fate would ultimately hinge on such subtleties, for its value came to rest largely on taxonomic status. To many people, the bird's worth depended on how high or low the scientific community placed the sparrow within the hierarchy of Latin names.

Despite the dusky's renown among birders, up to the time of Kale's visit little had been written about it. Beyond the brief description in the *Checklist* and a smattering of information in bird guides, almost all Kale knew about the bird came from the brief account published in 1932 by Arthur H. Howell in *Florida Bird Life*. According to Howell and other scattered accounts from the time, the breeding season lasted from April until early August, during which time the female laid two clutches of four or five eggs—somewhat elongated, with blunt ends, speckled in rich chestnut markings or in light browns, grays, and lavender, sometimes with a blob of solid color capping the egg's larger end. The birds bred in loose colonies with each male defending a definite nesting territory. The eggs hatched in twelve or thirteen days. Young birds remained in the nest for nine or ten days, and the chicks spent at least another twenty days after fledging under their parents' care. Two, possibly three, broods were reared in a season. Potential predators included raccoons and snakes and, in winter, harrier hawks. In high water, ants sometimes forced adults to abandon their nests.

The dusky gathered food throughout the marsh and sometimes flew a considerable distance to hunt for spiders and insects, as well as small crustaceans, on the exposed mud flats by the river. Nicholson watched one parent feed a fledgling an inch-long green worm. So scarce even today are the known details about the dusky's behavior that this single observation stands as a major contribution to the literature.

The dusky nested at least a mile and a half from the river where the broomgrass intermingled with black needle rush. It nested a few inches to two feet above firm ground. At the time of Nicholson's 1926 visit, occupied nests were built within about forty feet of each other—a distance that would steadily increase over the ensuing years of the dusky's decline. "The most beautiful nests of the dusky are built in burned-over clumps of switch-grass where the green fresh grass has grown about a foot high," he wrote. "In such sites the green grass is bent over to form a canopy with the entrance over the rim of the nest. These are extremely hard to find. . . . All nests built in pickleweed or switch-grass were made of grass, deeply cupped, and lined with finer grasses. Nests found in rushes were made of dead pieces of this coarse round-stemmed grass, lined with fine grass." In the grass Nicholson found the "cleverest and most artful nests which were marvels from a standpoint of concealment." On several occasions he walked right past them. He wrote, "A neat little trick, practiced in a number of instances, was the habit of scattering a few wisps of grass *carelessly* but directly, over the nest proper, thus shielding it from view above and giving it the decided effect of an incompleted nest, so deftly and craftily was this done." This camouflage hid the eggs from marauders. Once Nicholson walked near a nest, but thinking it in mid-construction, passed by. A few days later he again saw the same "incomplete" nest and, remembering the trick, lifted the grass and found four fresh eggs. Collectors had been raiding dusky nests on Merritt Island at least since the publication of F. M. Chapman's *Birds of Eastern North America* in 1911. Inspired by this account, collector O. W. Baynard found the first nest several years later.

Lacking glamour or size, the dusky seemed a mere detail in the marsh. Yet Kale was consumed by fascination for the bird. To him, the dusky was more than a variation on an evolutionary theme; the sparrow was a singular creation. The bird was not so much a creature of the present as a compilation of past evolution. The dusky's modern existence was defined by a journey that began thousands of years ago, like light from a distant star that is now visible. To see the sparrow only in the present was to ignore the dusky as living history.

Kale would have lingered longer in the marsh, but his fraternity brothers were impatient. After scribbling a few notes in his notebook, Kale climbed behind the steering wheel of the green Chevrolet, crossed back over the bridge, and headed south to Fort Lauderdale.

3

Apollo on the Moon

I n 1960 the National Aeronautics and Space Administration (NASA) began buying up North Merritt Island and adjoining Cape Canaveral for the site of the American spaceport—a land tract eventually to encompass the entire island range of the dusky seaside sparrow. Without knowing it, NASA had bought itself a species.

The island's inhospitality, as well as its proximity to the U.S. Air Force downrange tracking station at Point Jupiter, led NASA to choose this largely unknown, mosquito-infested stretch of Brevard County. Merritt Island beat out potential sites in Hawaii, Puerto Rico, and the Florida Keys. Without mosquitoes, by the late 1950s little undeveloped land on Merritt Island would have been left for NASA to buy. Word in Titusville at the time was that the recently deposed Cuban dictator Fulgencio Batista y Zaldivar had bought up much of Cape Canaveral and planned to create a new Miami Beach there.

By the time the buying spree was over, NASA had paid $72 million for about 140,000 acres. The boundaries of the Kennedy Space Center included much of Mosquito Lagoon; north to the barge canal; from the Indian River in the west to the Atlantic Ocean and Cape Canaveral in the east. Invoking the right of eminent domain, NASA bought out the dozens of families at "fair market value." Angered because the price they got for their land would not permit them to buy similar land on non-NASA parts of the island, many owners sued NASA. In almost every case, the jury dismissed the complaints. With the Soviet Union having already sent a man into space, this was no time for people to interfere with America's plan to put men on the moon. One woman who owned cultivated land on Merritt Island was forced to sell at $224 an acre; a year later, when she tried to buy a similar piece of land just outside NASA's boundaries, she found the price was $3000 an acre. A few years before the coming of the Kennedy Space Center, one family had moved from Savannah, Georgia, and bought land near Happy Lagoon, about four miles north of the future Vehicle Assembly Building. The husband and wife had come to cherish their new location. The Army Corps of Engineers, which purchased the land on NASA's behalf, promised that if they sold out and bought land north of Haulover Canal, five miles away, they need never worry about moving again. A few months later NASA expanded its boundaries, and the Corps forced the couple to sell again. They gave up and moved to Orlando. NASA also took in more than 2500 acres of citrus groves and leased them back to the former owners for an annual fee. Twenty beekeepers were allowed to keep hives on the island for $625 in annual dues, so the citrus trees would be pollinated. NASA also bought two cemeteries. The remains from one were dug up and reburied outside the space center boundaries; NASA allowed relatives to visit the other.

The space age had actually arrived in Florida more than a decade before the founding of NASA in 1959; and by the time of NASA's arrival, inroads had already been made into the dusky's habitat. Before NASA's time, the U.S. Air Force oversaw all space launches and had already built Launch Complexes 40, 41, and 42 on the Cape for the Titan 3Cs. A collection of intercontinental ballistic missiles stood a few miles farther south. Later came the pads for the old Redstone and Gemini launches. Records indicate that duskies may have historically nested along the western area of the Cape. Although no one can say for certain how many were nesting there when the Air Force arrived in the early 1950s, interconnecting roads between the launch complexes skirted several miles of dusky habitat. There early incursions had a minimal impact on the dusky. Nicholson estimated that DDT spraying for mosquitoes, however, had already eliminated up to 70 percent of the birds in the vicinity of Merritt Island between 1942 and 1953, leaving perhaps a couple thousand by the time spraying ended in the late 1950s. The sparrow had survived.

The operational heart of the new space center would be the gargantuan Vehicle Assembly Building, or VAB, where the Apollo rockets would be assembled before being rolled down a fifty-yard-wide "crawler way" to the launch pad. The Vehicle Assembly Building would stand on the south shore of Banana Creek where, a decade earlier, a nudist colony had flourished, along with a small fishing camp and a store that supplied bait, fishing hooks, and other essentials. These modern-day bathers contended with the mosquitoes by avoiding the area in the evening when the mosquitoes came out and during peak mosquito season, as no doubt did the Ais tribe which inhabited Merritt Island thousands of years before.

To prepare the ground for the Vehicle Assembly Building, a "palmetto plow" pulled up the plants by their roots and shook off the dirt. Saw-toothed bulldozers heaped the brush into pyres for burning. Earthmovers scooped nearly a half million tons of soft sand and muck from the foundation site. Hydraulic pumps on barges drew about half a cubic mile of sand and marl from the river for fill. Engineers unearthed huge slabs of petrified wood. One dredge spewed out the 100,000-year-old femur of a woolly mammoth estimated to have stood fifteen feet high. An herbivore, it fed on the dense growth of a marsh that may have borne remarkable similarities to the Merritt Island of recent times. The mammoths were a major source of food for some for the earliest roving hunter-gatherers that visited the island.

The foundation for the Vehicle Assembly Building was anchored with more than four thousand hollow steel pipes driven a hundred feet down to bedrock, filled with sand, and capped with cement. As many as ten large hydraulic pile drivers operated simultaneously throughout the night, illuminating North Merritt Island in a stadiumlike glow. Salt water in the ground reacted with the steel foundation to create an electrical current, leading to the creation of "the world's largest wet-cell battery." To prevent this electrolytic reaction—and the corrosion of the steel pilings—engineers connected large copper grounding wires to the pilings. On the cement foundation, three cranes erected the girders, consisting of enough steel to have built 48,000 automobiles. The Vehicle Assembly Building was so big that only by comparing it with familiar structures could NASA convey its size to the public. A structure rising 526 feet high (only 29 feet shorter than the Washington Monument) and longer than two football fields, the building would enclose 1.3 billion cubic feet—almost the equivalent of the Pentagon. Its bay door would be taller than the Statue of Liberty. When completed in 1964, the Vehicle Assembly Building reduced its surroundings to lilliputian scale. Roy Rogers once visited the building and quipped, "You could sure store a lot of hay in there."

About three miles east of the Vehicle Assembly Building, on a patch of marsh formerly inhabited by duskies, the massive Launch Complex 9A took shape. The circular two-hundred-acre site stood near the northern end of the Banana River, where the Canaveral Peninsula joins North Merritt Island. In the course of building the pad, draglines—cranelike machines with huge, toothed buckets—and dredges pulled fill from the river bottom, while bulldozers and other earth-movers heaped it into a pyramidal foundation nearly seventy feet high. Once the pad was completed, a cement sluiceway, as big as a gate of the Hoover Dam, ran from the base of the pad to deflect flames at lift-off.

Dredges cut a canal parallel to the roadbed for barges arriving from Louisiana, where the rocket boosters were built. A network of roads for carrying materials and workers to the construction sites was built through several areas of dusky habitat. NASA also constructed a causeway across the Indian River to Merritt Island, while a government railroad crossed the river just to the north. Later NASA built a four-mile-long runway, intended for the shuttle landing, across the interior of the island. The runway ended in a patch of former dusky habitat along Banana Creek.

Although construction of the space center pointed toward the future, everywhere the excavated land spoke of an ancient past. NASA engineers were not the first builders on Merritt Island. Near the pad stood a preexisting earthen mound. Designated Br 79 by the archaeologist who had described it in 1884, the mound yielded pottery dating back to about 2000 B.C.E., as well as one partial and two whole flint projectile points. Traces of a settlement from 1000 B.C.E. are now part of the mound on which Launch Pad 39A rests.

In one burial site from this period on the edge of NASA property and south of where Launch Complex 39 would stand, archaeologists discovered the skeletons of two hundred people arranged in a radial pattern with their heads pointing to the center of the mound like the spokes of a wheel. The centripetal configuration may have had celestial significance. Excavations of later Native American sites at the space center revealed European trade goods such as glass beads and iron implements that marked the time of the arrival of the Spanish.

Three thousand years ago, the entire area of the present Kennedy Space Center was inhabited by hunter-gatherers, banded in groups of less than fifty, who migrated from one locale to the next when they had depleted local food resources. They constructed temporary windbreaks for shelter and killed deer and other game with flint-tipped spears. Shellfish were an especially important food. The people also gathered snails from what was then apparently a freshwater river that skirted the island, as well as tiny, resplendent coquina along the beach and clams and oysters in the scattered lagoons. They revisited better campsites periodically and, as they consumed the shellfish, tossed the refuse underfoot. These shells accumulated over the years, forming mounds up to twenty-five feet high. These middens also contained bones from deer, alligators, turtles, fish, and birds, stone and shell tools, and other artifacts. Dozens of the shell-refuse traces still lie within the boundaries of Kennedy Space Center. On Merritt Island as elsewhere in Florida, many ancient middens have been excavated for roadbed fill.

The distribution of artifacts suggests that between 2000

B.C.E. and 1000 B.C.E. Merritt Island was thinly populated. Then, a major geological event occurred: a rise in sea level, perhaps spawned by a prolonged warming trend, or a storm of historic proportions, drove the ocean through the dunes and flooded the Indian River and its freshwater lagoons, creating a brackish backwater and making oysters and clams available over a wide new area. Semisedentary villagers settled in great numbers along the rich shores of Mosquito Lagoon and the rivers, often at the campsites of earlier hunter-gatherers. The pile-up of garbage and of history continued.

According to archaeologists, these new groups had a more complex culture than their predecessors. They buried their dead with elaborate rituals in sacred mounds and made better pottery than the earlier inhabitants, whose brittle, chalky pieces lacked plant fibers to hold the clay together. This advance, which began around the time of Christ, marked the beginning of what is called, in Brevard County, the Malabar period of Merritt Island.

The Vehicle Assembly Building and Launch Complex 39 are part of an extraordinary technological empire built on the remains of these ancient civilizations. By 1963 the skyline of Merritt Island had been transformed from one of low hammocks to one of huge geometric structures—among the largest human-made structures ever built. On hot summer days when the wind picked up, the industrial site appeared to be at the center of some apocalyptic event, as great clouds of dust and sand momentarily swallowed the buildings. In thunderstorms, the rising steel structure became a lightning rod. On August 3, 1965, as construction neared completion, construction worker Albert J. Treib was electrocuted when lightning struck Launch Complex 39 where he was working.

Throughout the building of the space center, mosquitoes continued to be a horrendous problem. During the peak summer mosquito season, workers would literally inhale the insects. Employees saturated their clothes and bodies with repellent, only to be delayed at the security gates the next morning with identity badges smeared beyond recognition by solvents in the insecticide.

Mosquitoes laid their eggs in the mud of the broomgrass flats surrounding the island exposed at low tide. The eggs incubated for three days, and then after a high tide or rain, hatched to liberate the larvae, which took flight as adults a week later. From spring through fall, with high tides or rain often following dry periods, the mosquitoes were at their worst. After a heavy rain, a single acre of Merritt Island salt marsh could produce fifty million mosquitoes.

Two species of mosquitoes dominated the marsh: *Aedes taeniorhynchus* and *Aedes sollicitans. A. taeniorhynchus* was a small black-and-white mosquito with distinct narrow white rings on the tarsi and proboscis, and dark wing scales. At dusk, newly emerged swarms began their migrations, flying up to twenty-five miles, usually downwind along the coast. Migrations, often in concert with the prevailing winds, were repeated two or three times a night. Then the brood settled down to feed, rest, and lay a batch of eggs. According to the *Handbook of Mosquito Control for Florida,* "This species is active chiefly after sunset. During the day they rest on the ground where grass or leaves offer a dark, moist, cool hiding place. However, if a stimulus reaches them, they will fly to it—which means if you go where they are in the daytime, they will be stimulated to bite you."

A. sollicitans, was larger, golden-brown, with wide pale bands on the tarsi and proboscis, wing scales mixed light and dark. Highly aggressive, according to the *Handbook,* "The adults usually rest during the day, but the females are persistent biters and will attack at any time of night or day." This species was especially aggressive and inflicted a painful, nasty bite. Although the saltwater mosquitoes are not generally associated with malaria, encephalitis, or other human epidemics, they can make life unendurable.

The insects were so numerous that they sometimes extinguished the lanterns used by fishermen who came to the island. During a mosquito outbreak, county mosquito-control inspectors from across the Indian River in Titusville recorded the density of the insects on Merritt Island in landings per minute, or LPMs. An inspector stood in the marsh while another clicked a hand-held counter, tabulating the number of the insects landing on his body. The count could easily reach 500 landings per minute. The aggressive mosquitoes often migrated in visible clouds across the Indian River and raided Titusville. A local saying went, "When mosquitoes die they go to Merritt Island; when they get hungry they come to Titusville."

By the summer of 1963, NASA had had enough, and the August 8 issue of *Spaceport News*, the in-house newspaper, announced that NASA,

> . . . normally a peace-loving agency, has declared war. But the earthbound enemy is one detested by all mankind—the ever-pestering mosquito. The "war," more exactly, is a co-operative program whereby Brevard County, the state . . . and the Air Force are teaming up to wage battle with mosquitoes in the 88,000-acre Merritt Island Launch Area. . . .The actual severity of the problem is almost unbelievable to all but natives of the area.

In the 1840s, the abundance of mosquitoes led the Honorable John Randolph of Virginia to stand before Congress, while the statehood of Florida was being debated, and proclaim that this "land of swamps, of quagmire, of frogs and alligators and mosquitoes" could never be developed without eliminating the mosquitoes. This was no exaggeration: as anyone knows who has truly contended with them, mosquitoes can inflict almost unbearable suffering. A mosquito-ridden wilderness, Florida was granted statehood in 1845. A century later, the state was still battling the problem.

Throughout the 1940s and 1950s Florida fought mosquitoes by drenching the marshes with DDT. Mixed with a light diesel fuel, it was sprayed from crop dusters or trucks that rumbled through the riverside towns. As a child in Florida, I often ran behind the truck in the wake of the gray clouds emanating from the nozzles at the back, for DDT had an almost candylike aroma. But the mosquitoes soon grew resistant to DDT. In fact, Brevard County was the first place in the world where resistance of saltwater mosquitoes to DDT was documented. Bombardment with copper, arsenic, and other chemicals worked for a while but depended on finding and dousing "hot spots" with the poisons.

As insecticides proved less effective, an entirely new approach to mosquito control was adopted. Rather than trying to destroy mosquitoes, the new technique sought to crimp the insect's prodigious reproductive capacity by eliminating breeding sites. This would entail building extensive dikes around marshes to permanently flood the land, transforming the marsh into a series of freshwater ponds, filled by rain or, in dry periods, with water pumped from the Indian River. The females would thus be denied the temporarily exposed ground for laying eggs. Concluded the *Spaceport News*, "Through the initiation of the master cooperative control plan the salt marsh mosquito may soon lose much of its notorious bite."

In the summer of 1963 the Joint Community Impact Coordination Committee (JCICC) drew up an agreement whereby NASA, the air force, and Brevard County would join forces in the eradication effort. This would cut the projected time required to complete diking from five years to three. With this vision on the drawing board, draglines moved into the marsh. Where the earth was too soft to support their weight, a temporary roadway of timber planking was set down. Machines disemboweled the salt marsh.

Many of the Merritt Island marshes—including those along northern stretches of the Indian River, which held the major concentrations of duskies—had been partially diked for the benefit of Titusville even before NASA's arrival, but the island remained open and mosquito-ridden. In time, nearly two hundred additional miles of four-foot-high dikes, encompassing 14,000 acres, divided the Merritt Island salt marsh into rice-paddy-like cells, ranging in size from a few acres to several hundred. NASA soon won its biggest battle in the war against mosquitoes.

Most people who grew up in that part of Florida, as I did, would find it difficult to be an apologist for mosquitoes. But a few points should be made about them. If humans eliminated all mosquitoes tomorrow, it would remain to be seen if the world would be better off, for there is no telling how many species would be eliminated with them. One might argue that the mosquito is the wilderness's most powerful ally because it has protected some of earth's most pristine places from human encroachment. For a time, the insects did so on Merritt Island.

In his 1972 treatise, *The Mosquito: Its Life, Activities, and Impact on Human Affairs*, J. D. Gillett catalogued the numerous atrocities of this insect against humanity, from deadly outbreaks of malaria to yellow fever. But he concluded with a warning:

> If, as seems likely, man shortly succeeds in killing off many of his larger fellow-tetrapods, and the elephant, gorilla, whale and crocodiles become almost legendary figures of the past, he is not so easily going to dispose of the mosquitoes. . . . I

think the present time may well go down in history as the period when man sought to conquer and control nature as if he himself were something apart, when the ignorance of the nineteenth century was replaced by the arrogance of the twentieth. But I question the whole present-day attitude that defines progress and civilization as conquests over nature. Progress can come only from an understanding of and an attempt to co-operate with the forces of nature in the full realization that we ourselves as well as the mosquitoes that bite us are molded by these very forces and are as inseparable from them as the clouds from the sky.

As construction of the space center neared completion, and with the mosquito population dramatically reduced, once sparsely populated Merritt Island was temporary home to seven thousand construction workers—in addition to several thousand employees of NASA. Old neighborhoods in Titusville and surrounding communities vanished, and a city grew. Old-timers disappeared as transient specialists moved in. Many of the new residents of Brevard County were skilled at maintaining the space complex, but they hardly knew a palmetto from a pompano. The benefits were compelling—better paying jobs, better schools, and a future as a part of the space age. But these did not come without a price. Titusville pediatrician Ronald C. Erbs claimed, "Before coming to this area, I did not see ulcers in children, except for rare examples. It is my opinion that the life generated by the Space Program was basically unhealthy for the families of space personnel. . . . These tensions then were felt by the children, and since the problems were not usually discussed, the children had no outlet for these emotions, leading to the development of ulcers." Divorce rates also soared. Titusville and the environs of Merritt Island were no longer southern backwaters. Long traffic delays became the curse of Titusville and all who lived there. To meet the demands for recreation and provide an outlet for a frenetic society, NASA established Playalinda Beach on the northern shores of the space center. Much to NASA's chagrin, nude sun worshippers routinely gathered along the shore—within sight of Launch Complex 39—and only yards beyond a sign posted on the beach: Nude Bathing Prohibited Under Florida State Law.

In 1963 NASA turned over about 57,000 acres of buffer zone surrounding the launch areas to the Bureau of Sports Fisheries and Wildlife, the bureaucratic ancestor of the U.S. Fish and Wildlife Service. At the urging of the nationally known ornithologist and wildlife photographer Allan Cruickshank, who lived in the nearby town of Rockledge, the area was designated the Merritt Island National Wildlife Refuge. NASA later added land to the refuge for a total of 126,000 acres. In time the refuge would expand to 140,000 acres.

"Four years of herculean toil by architects, engineers, and construction workers . . . transformed North Merritt Island wasteland into the operation launch base of today," reads the official history of the space center. "Wildlife continues to inhabit the Refuge apparently oblivious or inured to rocket blast-offs, the daily presence of thousands of workers and heavy vehicular traffic . . . The Bureau permits controlled duck hunting in the Lagoon and in 25 blinds erected along the Indian River shore. Hunters pay $3 per day for use of a blind. It is the only spot on earth where they could shoot ducks in the shadow of a Moon Rocket."

4

Mosquitoes

In NASA's early days, diking was pursued with the fervor of Manifest Destiny. The frontiers of technology would be extended to the uninhabited fringes of Brevard County. Local Mosquito Control employees became virtual heroes, relating their heroics in Titusville bars late into the night. Remarkably, throughout the early days of Merritt Island's transformation by diking, almost no one at NASA or elsewhere in Brevard County had ever heard of a dusky seaside sparrow.

Diking effectively reduced the mosquito population, but side effects were profound. By creating permanent impoundments behind the dikes, the entire salt marsh flooding regimen was transformed. The broomgrass could not withstand constant flooding and was replaced by thick shrubs. Impounding also changed the salt marsh to mostly fresh water, as the brackish Indian and Banana Rivers were kept at bay and rain filled the impoundments. This change to fresh water encouraged the growth of cattails. The cattails and shrubby growth, in turn, ushered in their own animal clientele. The heretofore scarce red-winged blackbird became common on Merritt Island, as did the aggressive boat-tailed grackle. The land of broomgrass and open salt marsh became a series of shallow, stagnant freshwater ponds.

Concern expressed for the dusky came as early as 1955, when Rubert J. Longstreet warned in the *Florida Naturalist* that mosquito control would harm the dusky. The following year, egg collector Donald Nicholson wrote to the Bureau of Sports Fisheries that the "once-famous breeding ground of the dusky seaside sparrow" had been transformed and "in my opinion, it may not be too long before this very restricted species will become extremely rare. It may entirely disappear. . . ." In the spirit of a true egg collector, he told the service, "Should the National Museum be in need of a few more skins of the dusky seaside sparrow, certainly *now* is the time to get them. This bird has decreased greatly in numbers during the past 15 years."

The first to actually document the profound impact of diking on the dusky was Charles Trost, a taciturn graduate student who came to Merritt Island in 1962 to research his master's degree in wildlife biology from the University of Florida, Gainesville. The young scholar looked forward to conducting an objective scientific study on the effects of impoundments on birdlife in Brevard County.

A 1962 article in the *Orlando Sentinel* chronicled Charles and his wife Lucy Trost's arrival. Color photographs depict a handsome couple, she with blond bangs and a ponytail; he with dark hair combed back at a slight angle, wearing thick-rimmed glasses and grinning. One photograph bears the caption, "Bird counters Chuck and Lucy Trost prepare lunch on the marshes." It was May, and Lucy was dressed in a sleeveless red pullover and Chuck, as he was known, in a short-sleeved plaid shirt. The article captured the adventurous, pioneering spirit that brought the couple to Merritt Island. Driving around the island in an old red Volkswagen with a boat lashed atop, the newly married Chuck and Lucy Trost seemed to be living the brightest moment of their lives.

According to the newspaper account, "Chuck can spot a bird at an incredible distance and identify it immediately. And he can spot the little shore and ground birds where the layman would only see a brush or sand patch. Chuck also runs a test of salinity on the impounded ponds and reports that they are almost completely fresh now in many instances where the rainwater has flushed all the salt out." The paper called him a "wilderness explorer." Wilderness though Merritt Island may have seemed, before Trost could enter NASA property he had to get a National Agency Check by documenting good citizenship and filling out a blizzard of attached forms, as enumerated in a letter from the colonel in charge of the restricted area: "DD Fm 48 in quint; DD Fm 48-1 in quint; Fingerprint chart; AFMTC Fm 45; Ltr MTF 7 Aug 61, subj: Req for Badge, CCMTA; Ist Ind MTIPA 7 Aug 61, same subj." Trost understood that it was only a couple of years after the Soviets had launched Sputnik. NASA, behind in the space race, didn't need any communist spies in its midst.

Trost's study had actually been conceived by Maurice Provost, director of the Entomological Research Center under the Florida State Board of Health, in Vero Beach. The center (later renamed the Florida Medical Entomology Laboratory) was the driving force behind mosquito eradication efforts in Florida. Provost and his staff conducted mosquito research, tracked the spread of mosquito-borne diseases, and laid the scientific groundwork for diking the marshes of Brevard County. The center also recommended to mosquito-control directors in various counties the best ways to eradicate mosquitoes.

Provost had received his Ph.D. in zoology from Iowa State University in 1947, under the well-known wetlands ecologist Paul Errington, whose deep appreciation for marshes undoubtedly influenced his student. Provost was genuinely concerned with the long-term impacts of diking in Florida, not only upon the dusky, but upon other forms of life in the marsh. The year after his graduation, while director of research at the Entomological Research Center, Provost wrote, "Thinking people, while granting that mosquitoes are undesirable, will also see beyond the mosquitoes. They will realize that the infinitely intricate pattern of soil, water, plant, and animal . . . has values which dwarf on a grandiose scale the mere elimination of mosquitoes. Therefore they can adopt but one logical attitude towards mosquito control: it is desirable and yet in the perspective of value and time it must be practiced with utmost care." Provost felt that no form of mosquito control, farming, or forest management, for that matter, could ever be dreamed up "which will not tamper with food-chains or ecological balances . . . all purposeful manipulation of habitats and populations is unnatural, leaving us therefore only ends to judge and not means. Having selected and justified an end, we can only hope to achieve it by such means as are least disturbing to natural processes and least prejudicial to an infinity of natural production."

At once philosophical and scientific, Provost's conservation ethic defied easy classification. He held membership in the Sierra Club, The Nature Conservancy, and the Environmental Defense Fund, and had received a special conservation award from the Florida Audubon Society. In his other life, Provost was president of the Florida Anti-Mosquito Association, many of whose members viewed organizations such as the Sierra Club as ballyhooing environmentalists. A rare combination of scholar, administrator, politician, and conservationist, Provost wrote papers on aspects of mosquitoes ranging from the effect of relative humidity on their night flight to the biomechanics of their motion.

As early as 1959 Provost had begun to speculate about the impact of diking on the dusky, but at the time considered it a "fact yet to be established." In 1960, when Paul F. Springer, Chief of the Section of Wetland Ecology at Patuxent Wildlife Research Center in Maryland, queried Provost about the long-term effects of diking on the Florida salt marsh, Provost, after checking with a local ornithologist, admitted that the dusky was in serious trouble:

> Yesterday I had a lengthy phone conversation with the one man who knows Brevard County birds like a book—mainly about the dusky seaside sparrow. In his estimation, mosquito control is about to exterminate that bird. From the thousands that were in the marshes across from Titusville some 20 or 30 years ago, he estimates there are now some 25 precariously located birds. I have no reason to doubt this excellent ornithologist. He attributed the catastrophic drop to DDT spraying in the early post-war years, and it is true that this area did get some of the most intensive . . . spraying in the late forties. . . . He tells me the dusky feeds almost exclusively on the ground—probably spiders and insects mostly. The DDT bath could well have reduced its food drastically enough to decimate the dusky's numbers. And now, he says, flooding the marsh is finishing the job of extermination. . . . As for [the St. Johns] colonies of duskies, he couldn't be sure because the terrain where they occur is now so swamped with rattlesnakes neither he nor anyone else apparently cares to explore it. . . . I will shortly get with the mosquito-control director in Brevard County and see if a dusky seaside sparrow "refuge" can't be set up in the marshes across from Titusville.

It is not clear who the "excellent ornithologist" is that

Provost referred to in his letter, but probably Donald Nicholson, who had echoed some of these sentiments in an earlier letter. But shortly after Provost conveyed this discouraging news, he heard a totally different appraisal of the dusky situation from Allan Cruickshank. Provost wrote back to Springer: "I know you'll be glad to hear [Cruickshank] was not at all sure that impoundment was hurting this species. He said that . . . around those big Titusville impoundments . . . he had seen more duskies along the dikes than he'd ever seen before in one day!" Actually, Provost had Cruickshank's impression at secondhand and perhaps something was lost in the translation, for Cruickshank must have understood as well as anyone the impact of diking on the dusky. If he saw more sparrows that day, it was probably only because diking had made the marsh more accessible, and therefore, the birds initially easier to find.

As both a public servant and a scientist, Provost occupied a professional niche colored by political considerations. And if he skillfully used his quasi-political role to advance the cause of his science, he also used his scientific credentials to advance his politics. Provost not only designed Trost's study to the last detail and planned to be on the thesis committee, but also obtained funding from the U.S. Fish and Wildlife Service to support it. In fact, Provost's organization, not Trost, would be the contractor and therefore control the money. Trost would be paid $275 a month for three years, working on weekends during school and full-time during the summer. He would also be given $1500 a year for traveling expenses. On his arrival, Trost had an uneasy feeling that his research had been choreographed; that the conclusions to his study had already been drawn.

Among other things, Provost wanted to make a strong case for diking, for he firmly believed that when it came to controlling mosquitoes, diking was a lesser evil than pesticides. Besides, diking not only controlled mosquitoes, it offered other benefits—in particular the creation of freshwater impoundments for waterfowl. Waterfowl would be a powerful ally in the argument for diking; ducks had always come in prodigious numbers to North Merritt Island, even in its natural state, but year-round freshwater impoundments throughout Brevard County would make the whole county a magnet for ducks. Ducks were big business. Ducks could be shot, bagged, and eaten. A huge gun-toting political constituency followed them. Duck stamps raised revenue. County commissioners and congressmen cherished duck hunting. From a management perspective, Merritt Island would be a dream. Roads atop the dikes would provide easy access for wildlife agents keeping tabs on bag limits. "Impoundments," Provost wrote, "are absolutely made-to-order for waterfowl management." Provost also knew that impoundments created habitat for beautiful wading birds such as egrets, which were popular with bird-watchers. If the public saw mosquito control as synonymous with waterfowl habitat and bird-watching, the battle against any potential opposition—in the press or elsewhere—would be more easily won. Trost could make it happen by establishing the scientific connection between ducks and diking. The young student was expected to scientifically prove that impoundments, while effective in eliminating mosquitoes, had transformed Brevard County into duck paradise. Provost wanted Trost to quantify these "improvements" and make an irrefutable case for the "ecological" benefits of diking.

With a genuine scientific curiosity about salt marsh species, Provost resisted every impulse to adopt a view of the world in which the only measure of nature's value was its utility. "To the average person this vast intertidal acreage is wasteland and it undoubtedly is signalized as the ultimate in 'improvement' to see this terrain converted to residential or industrial real estate. . . . There is then no champion for the natural and undisturbed intertidal land except for the rare naturalist with an esthetic sense unalloyed with utilitarianism," he wrote.

But while decrying the lack of a "champion" to fight for preserving the salt marsh, Provost himself then fell victim to the "utilitarian" philosophy he preached against. In this same paper Provost stated that "81% of Florida's intertidal land had low or negligible waterfowl value," and he argued for "improving" the marshes by impounding them to convert the barren expanses into bird-rich impoundments: "Impounded salt marshes become havens for ducks. . . . Hunters have gotten their limits of ducks readily on certain impoundments. Management possibilities for duck production or harvest are excellent. The main deterrent to management of the unreclaimed Florida salt marsh is that it is so often, so long, and so unpredictably a virtual desert."

Although Provost was the intellectual driving force behind the study, Trost worked almost daily with Jack Salmela, the amiable director of Brevard County Mosquito Control. Salmela, who consulted with Provost when necessary, oversaw all mosquito-control activities in the county. It was Salmela who led NASA's war against mosquitoes. While Trost saw Provost as "an intellectual and a scholar" he viewed Salmela as a "local boy who made good." Salmela was also an avid duck hunter. Militaristic in his antimosquito fervor, if Salmela sometimes came across as a muleteer to his employees, he was more often viewed as a fervent and honest public servant. A fighter pilot in the China-Burma-India campaign of 1944, after the war Salmela returned to his native Brevard County and worked as a pilot for Mosquito Control, spraying DDT from a biplane. He often saved the county money by landing his Steerman aircraft on an eighteen-foot-wide roadbed of Highway A1A along the coast. Given that the Steerman aircraft had no front window, this was a feat. He would reload with pesticides, avoiding the time and expense of flying to the regular landing strip at Valkaria nearly forty miles away. Taking off from the highway, he had to swoop under a powerline before climbing steeply over the next. Once while spraying in Melbourne, Salmela clipped a radio communication tower with a wing. The aircraft plummeted sixty feet, nose first into the ground. Dazed, burned, and bleeding from the face, Salmela struggled from the flaming wreckage, limped to a nearby highway, and hitched a ride into town. Here was a man with the stuff to fight mosquitoes.

Salmela offered himself as Trost's virtual servant for the study, sharing his knowledge of the local terrain and putting Mosquito Control's planes and boats at Trost's disposal for surveying the impoundments. Over time, the Salmelas and Trosts became close friends. Chuck, Lucy, Jack, and his wife, Helen, as well as their three children, occasionally went camping together in the St. Johns River Valley. Trost developed an innocent crush on Salmela's beautiful sixteen-year-old daughter Joy, and Trost became something of a second father and a mentor to Salmela's youngest son Bobby. The elder Salmela valued these friendships, and encouraged Bobby to hang around with the graduate student. Bobby was quiet and thoughtful, and, like his father, a little nervous. On weekends Bobby often accompanied Trost to the marsh, learning the broader principles of ecology. Trost used to tell him things like, "In nature, you've got to look at the whole picture, Bobby, beyond your neighborhood, town, or time. Man measures change in days; nature measures it in centuries."

A few months after his arrival, Trost accompanied Cruickshank and Cruickshank's friend Lon Ellis to the marsh. Handicapped by polio since his youth, Ellis often had to struggle through the marsh in rubber hip boots, pointing out where duskies once had been. "Ever since diking began, the duskies have been rapidly disappearing from the island," Ellis told Trost. "In the spring, they used to sing everywhere in the marshes from the broomgrass. But now the broomgrass is gone and has been replaced by freshwater plants."

Until this meeting, Trost had focused almost exclusively on the increased waterfowl. This visit to the marsh profoundly changed his thinking. Trost was so taken by the unpublicized plight of the sparrow that he began studying the dusky on his own time. Why should he sing only the praise of waterfowl, which could easily be found elsewhere, when the success had been achieved at the expense of the unique dusky? But even as the soft-spoken Trost began to realize the extent of the transformation wrought by diking, he said nothing publicly. He continued to nurture his friendship with the Salmelas. But for the first time Trost understood how political concerns, personal friendships, and potential conflicts had begun to insidiously undermine his scientific independence. He came to question the cause for which he felt Mosquito Control had enlisted him—to provide a justification for destruction of the salt marshes. In time, he came to believe that a pervasive greed, not Mosquito Control specifically, was ultimately responsible for the "ecological rape" of the salt marsh. It seemed that everyone had an ulterior motive. Beyond the pressures of the space race, Trost believed that powerful individuals with financial motives drove the relentless diking: wealthy speculators, allied with county commissioners, knew that land values around Titusville would soar once mosquitoes were eliminated.

Trost became so preoccupied with the dusky that he often went to the marsh and painfully documented the sparrow's demise. He typed his observations on log sheets: "We censused [an] impoundment from 9 to 12 noon. . . . A dusky nest with four young was found during the count"; a few days later at the same area "a lot of ducks and coots had come in. No duskies were seen." A short time later, Trost, several others, and a NASA representative went out to North Canaveral Impoundment to see the effect of the Saturn launch on wildlife. Trost wrote, "We were about two miles from the missile and when it was shot off the sky was full of pintails which had previously been hidden from view. There were about 2500 of them in the impoundment. Many of them dropped back into the marsh after one circular flight; the rest sat down in the Banana River while we were present. Almost everything except coots flew when the noise hit us. Most coots dashed for cover, but the noise was not unbearably loud and they were soon feeding normally again. Some birds may be conditioned to this; for example, I saw some redwings take off after the flash and before the noise had reached us. We told [the NASA representative] that there was no obvious danger to wildlife where the C-1 missiles now are. I told him that when the C-5 pads are in (one of which will be in the Mosquito Lagoon marsh) they may find that a siren blast before the shot will save quite a few ducks. Everyone seemed to agree with this idea."

On March 8, 1963, Trost "went to the marsh until dark, and the duskies were singing for the first time this year." As Provost and others had predicted, waterfowl found the freshwater impoundments irresistible. Where once there was only a vast and quiet salt marsh stretching across a glistening green horizon, dotted by numerous natural ponds and inhabited year-round by only two highly specialized species of birds, now there were endless series of freshwater impoundments alive with splashing waterfowl. Migrating season by season along the dikes and into the impoundments, plants that were strangers to the traditional salt marsh began to take over, especially wax myrtle and the exotic Brazilian peppertree, its turpentine-scented evergreen foliage hung with clusters of bright red drupes in midwinter. The woody growth colonizing the dikes attracted new predators such as snakes and rats. "We again banded dusky seaside sparrows from 7:30 A.M. to 2:00 P.M," wrote Trost of one such dike. "We captured [and banded] five new birds. There were three new redwing nests found on the dike and one was in the middle of the marsh—in a spartina bush. A mottled duck and nine ducklings were seen on this marsh. The other mottled nest still had eggs." But the dusky was now becoming ever harder to find:

> July 15: I looked for seaside sparrows west of Indian River City all day—no luck. The place they were found last year had been burned over during the winter—possibly they are in the vicinity.

> July 16: I went back to the same area on this date, but could not find the sparrow.

On July 30, the normally protective Trost, under enormous pressure from a professor at the University of Florida who wanted a skin for the university's collection, netted a dusky in the vicinity of Mosquito Lagoon. According to records at the Florida Museum of Natural History, the following year Trost captured three more on Merritt Island—two of them females. Trost planned to use them in physiology experiments to study how their kidneys regulated the high salt intake from the marsh—a topic in which he planned to pursue his Ph.D. Two of the duskies died in captivity. When Trost was later accepted into a Ph.D. program at the University of California, Los Angeles to pursue a related topic, he curtailed the experiment. He drove back to the Merritt Island marsh and released the surviving sparrow. The skins of the others now lie in drawers at the museum.

Even as Trost continued to visit the marsh, the machines

were at work: "Lucy and I searched the grass in the path of draglines which are making a railroad bed through the fresh marsh. We were looking for dusky nests, as they would be destroyed by the draglines." Obvious changes—standing water, loss of nesting vegetation and ground for foraging—transformed the marsh. A large alligator, which Trost had seen on numerous occasions sunning himself, "was not in its normal sunning spot and grass was growing in the marsh where it used to lie." Nearby, "fishermen reported a big fish kill in one of the sloughs of this same vast, new impoundment—probably from water loss."

With changes in vegetation, Trost witnessed firsthand the changes in the animal community. The dusky had evolved to live among its traditional predators—rice rats, four species of snakes, ants, and raccoons. But the fresh water brought the large and aggressive pig frog, which ate nestlings, and ever increasing numbers of boat-tailed grackles and red-winged blackbirds, which took up residence in the bushes growing on the dikes.

Trost did not limit his forays to the planned study areas but frequently ventured to look for duskies in the St. Johns. He also continued taking Salmela's son Bobby with him to the Merritt Island marsh but found the trips increasingly painful, for it was the boy's father who was at the vanguard of the diking. Yet the friendship between the Trosts and the Salmelas endured. When Chuck and Lucy returned to Pennsylvania to visit family, they often spoke on the telephone or corresponded with the Salmelas on matters concerning the study. "You have been a great comfort," Salmela once wrote to Lucy, whom he came to adore. In letters to her Salmela would sign off, "With love."

Writing up the results of his study in 1964, Trost concluded that diking was, indeed, good for waterfowl; impoundments had increased the number of waterfowl and wading birds sevenfold. But, wrote Trost, "the same conditions which were ideal for water birds, were undesirable for the once abundant dusky seaside sparrow."

Numbers alone tell but one dramatic chapter in the marsh's transformation and the dusky's decline. An estimated two thousand pairs of duskies had once lived on Merritt Island. Nicholson speculated that by 1957 DDT, a residual poison, had reduced this number by 70 percent, leaving about six hundred pairs of duskies. Over the next five years—the use of DDT had been discontinued after 1952 because of resistant mosquitoes—the Merritt Island marshes were completely and permanently impounded. By the time Trost conducted his study between 1961 and 1963, he found only about seventy pairs in four colonies. In other words, if DDT had reduced the population by 70 percent, the population was then reduced by another 90 percent after diking. Provost's statement to Springer that "flooding the marsh is finishing the job of extermination" would turn out to be a colossal understatement.

In his study Trost concluded, "The bunchgrass [*Spartina*] in which they nested was not able to germinate under conditions of continuous inundation. As a consequence the existing stand became very sparse and eventually disappeared. . . . Special consideration should be given clapper rails and seaside sparrows, both of which appear to be forced out from lack of adequate food and cover in extensive impounded areas."

As a result of his findings, Trost recommended building dikes a hundred yards or so away from the river, leaving a fringe of remaining marsh. This lower portion of the marsh would not raise mosquitoes anyway, since this area was inundated almost daily. The buffer zone of marsh would also have protected the dikes from storm surges. While not ideal, the compromise was better than nothing: some of the original vegetation would be saved, along with the intertidal snails, crustaceans and other food the dusky relied on. Trost also suggested building adjustable gates into the dikes so the marshes could be flooded during peak mosquito season, then drained for the rest of the year for the dusky. In this way, the needs of mosquito control and conservation of the duskies could both be met with little cost to the other. His recommendations were ignored.

Like Trost, Provost also believed that this so-called rotational management, or multipurpose use, was compatible with the duskies' survival. But as Provost saw it, politics stood in the way of implementing Trost's recommendations: "mosquito control impoundments *could* be managed for multipurpose values—[but] . . . however well-intended mosquito-control directors are—and you couldn't find [a] better conservationist than Jackie Salmela—their mission is mosquito control and that is where their tax dollars have to go."

Although Salmela had expressed concern that "impoundments are definitely changing the present habitat of the dusky seaside sparrow," as the director of Mosquito Control, he had his own worries. Working under a contract that had to be renewed annually by the county commissioners, Salmela was under enormous pressure to control mosquitoes however he could. Too many public complaints about mosquitoes would cost him his job. Salmela could either completely accommodate the dusky or he could effectively fight mosquitoes—but not both. Salmela personally loathed mosquitoes and once wrote in a letter to a colleague, "I just can't bear the sight of large rafts of pupae and millions of newly hatched adults without doing something to kill them."

An angry Trost resisted the temptation to go public with his concerns, as he knew that, given the political realities, this would only make life difficult for Salmela and Provost. Trost decided to remain silent—a decision he would regret.

He personally mourned for the duskies almost every day he went to the marsh. With the impoundments across Merritt Island completed, in 1969 Provost addressed a conference in Florida and cited Trost's research on waterfowl: "On the basis of exhaustive statistical analysis of voluminous data, we can summarize our finding with the simple statement that for the birds common enough to yield meaningful data, seven species were unaffected, six were hurt, and twenty-two were helped by marsh flooding." Along with the duskies, also "hurt" were the red-breasted mergansers, horned grebes, pelicans, cormorants, anhingas, and clapper rails.

By 1965 Trost had emerged as the undisputed authority on the rare sparrow. Lucy got pregnant unexpectedly and Trost abandoned the field work to enter his Ph.D. program at UCLA. In 1968 he accepted a teaching post at Idaho State University, in Pocatello. A short time later, a shattered Jack Salmela called him on the telephone and said that Bobby had been killed in Vietnam in a mortar attack on his camp between Khe Sanh and Hue. Jack said that Bobby had recently written that Vietnam would be a beautiful country if not for the war. His mother had planned to send him a camera for his upcoming birthday to take pictures of the countryside.

Trost was deeply saddened, not only for Bobby, but for Jack. Salmela was so angry about his son's death that at first he refused to have Bobby buried in military uniform. But after the undertaker had prepared the body, Salmela thought his son looked so handsome in formal dress that he consented. Bobby's grave is in Melbourne, Florida, and his name became among the earliest etched into the dark granite face of the Vietnam War Memorial in Washington, D.C. Trost could hardly believe how quickly the boy who had once accompanied him to the marshes had grown into a young man, and how swiftly and violently he had been taken away.

Trost never did publish anything about the benefit of diking to waterfowl, only about its detriment to the dusky. In 1968 he wrote about the dusky in the authoritative Arthur Cleveland Bent series on the life histories of North American birds. In the account Trost, for the first time, openly accused Mosquito Control of destroying the dusky on Merritt Island. The slim entry also remains the definitive scientific account of the life history of the sparrow—all eleven pages.

5

If Only

I first met Charles Trost in the summer of 1990 over a cup of black coffee in a small diner on the main street of Pocatello. Twenty-five years had passed since he had worked with the dusky. Although many details of the time eluded him, his emotions were fresh and strong. Trost slowly traced his index finger around a fresh coffee ring on the formica tabletop and said, "For the rest of my life I will regret that I did not speak out for the dusky. I knew what was happening, but I was too young and inexperienced to know what to do. If only I had spoken out, maybe things would have been different. That was a long time ago, but the regret doesn't go away; it grows."

He said that he and Lucy had long since divorced; their son was now twenty-six. He said he had lost touch with most of the people he had known on Merritt Island. He handed me a bundle of his old notes and maps from the glove compartment of his car and told me he still treasured them.

When I told him I would be going to Merritt Island the next day to do some research, Trost asked if Salmela was still alive. I said I had spoken with Salmela just a few days earlier. Trost said to please tell him hello.

The following day I was back in my Brevard County hotel room, studying the notes and annotated maps Trost had given me in Pocatello. Carrying photocopies of the material with me, I drove across the bridge over the Indian River and to the highway through the heart of Merritt Island National Wildlife Refuge. Two miles into the refuge, I passed a Toyota truck stopped at roadside. An anhinga, wings spread, had collided with the truck and had somehow gotten pinned beneath a windshield wiper. Beyond the truck rose the Vehicle Assembly Building, and north of that, the gantry at 39A. I turned onto a side road and parked near an impoundment known as Black Point. A green nylon knapsack slung over my shoulder, I followed the well-worn Allan Cruickshank Trail—named in honor of his getting NASA to designate land for the refuge—along a dike to the western edge of the Indian River. Along the way, I searched out the spots where Trost had written "duskies" on a map. Phalanxes of ducks covered the impoundments. A boat-tailed grackle did a balancing act atop a tall signpost. A red-winged blackbird sang loudly from a bush growing a few yards off the dike, and an eastern meadowlark wafted by. I sat down at the edge of the impoundment and looked around. I pulled out a small microscope I sometimes carry. I drew a small amount of water from the marsh into an eyedropper, spotted it on a slide and placed a thin rectangle of cover glass over it, then slipped it under the clamps beneath the turret. I looked at the water. I wrote in my journal:

> One of the great joyful secrets of life is that most of it remains unseen. From the small organisms living in the lush forests of the living room carpet to the myriad creatures that

call a square centimeter of the marsh home, the large majority of life eludes us, everyday, all of our lives. Back-lit by the evening sun on the mirror, the drop of marsh water became a swirling and teeming ocean of life—radiolaria, their edges illuminated by refractive blues and sea-glass-greens, rolled by like pockmarked meteorites through space. A purple peanut-shell-shaped bacteriumlike organism with a long tail scooted curiously through the circular window of the lens. Diatoms shuffled forward and backward like bumper cars, their geometrical external skeletons crosshatched and lined. Through these lenses one is drawn into the inner sanctum of life, where creatures by sheer exuberance and variety add new perspective to our crude clumsy daily plodding through the world. Life here on Merritt Island is as rich as ever. It has merely changed.

There were mosquitoes, but only a few, toward late afternoon. I caught one on the knee of my cotton pants and crushed it lightly, then placed it under the turret. Ten times magnified, it was exquisite as a mayfly. Its variegated wings spread out in overlapping oval panels of silk. The wing scales, an alternating light and dark checkerboard arrangement, gave it away as *Aedes sollicitans*. The back edges of the wings were lined with a short, fine, even row of bristles. The seven segments of the abdomen were covered in a cast of golden brown pallor. It was a female—I could have deduced that because it was biting me—with a long, smoothly rounded proboscis extending beyond the pair of antennae curving outward like elephant tusks.

I emptied the remaining Gatorade from my canteen into the dry abyss of my mouth as a great southern white butterfly alighted on the tip of my moccasins. Its white wings flickered in the sunlight, the sooty edges of its forewings creating a scalloped pattern against the white. There was a time when huge streams of great southern whites migrated up and down the Florida coast. The larvae of the butterfly depended on pickleweed for food. The adults often traveled corridors farther inland to feed on lantana and *Eugenia* shrubs. The butterflies fed once a day for about forty-five minutes, the females in the morning and the males in the afternoon. But this was the only butterfly I saw all day. They used to descend on the Merritt Island marshes in droves. In 1984 Erik Tetens Nielsen of the Sherwood Hammock Biological Laboratory in Fort Pierce, described the migrations in Florida in a paper he sent to William Opp, manager of the Office of Entomology, in Jacksonville: "What in old days made the white butterflies well known to most people was, of course, their migrations," he wrote, describing the steady flight of thousands of butterflies, all fluttering a few feet above the ground and heading the same direction—without so much as stopping for feeding, rest, or mating. He estimated one migration near Cape Canaveral in the spring of 1954—the same year Kale had first visited Merritt Island—to have included up to one million butterflies. "All this belongs to the past," he lamented, then went on to blame as among the causes for the decline, the impoundment for mosquito control of the marshes. "Let us face the truth," he concluded, ". . . the remaining stretches of natural vegetation are fast vanishing. This is what is called progress, and it will always win. Therefore, I think that any effort to bring back the butterfly migrations are wasted. Even if it should be possible to do it, I have serious doubts whether it would be a success. To old-timers the butterflies were something to enjoy to see, but to the people who now have invaded the coast they would just be a nuisance. Think of the panic if an outbreak occurred in a trailer park or a shopping center with tens of thousands of butterflies milling around—it is an awe-inspiring experience. There would be an outcry beseeching all authorities to come with insecticide to get rid of the damned bugs."

I lingered in the marsh almost until nightfall; one of the

most beautiful times to be there is sunset, when all the birds get ready to roost for the night and evacuate the skies for the marshes. Trost had told me evening was one of his favorite times there. The slow-stroking wings of herons and wood storks fanned the darkening sky as if descending silently from heaven, before alighting in trees and transfixing themselves into statuettes. Across the Indian River, a sky supple as purple candle wax melted onto the horizon. A trio of egrets, their slender legs jutting just beyond their tail feathers, swam through the misty blue light. All the duskies would have been in their nests by now.

Returning to my hotel in Titusville later that night, I trudged into the lounge adjacent to the inn, sat at the bar, and perused a pocket guide on butterflies. I asked the bartender for a Coors. She clanked it down in front of me, announced that she was married, and waited for me to pay. I wrote Trost a postcard—a photograph of earth viewed from the moon. I thanked him for the time he had spent with me in Pocatello. I got sleepy after half a beer and walked across the parking lot to my room at the Space Shuttle Inn.

6

Endangered

In 1966, six weeks after the lunar craft *Surveyor 3* scooped up dust to test for evidence of life on the moon, Congress passed the first law in history to protect endangered species on earth. The law came none too soon for the dusky. After months of searching, Trost had found only about seventy pairs of the sparrows in four widely isolated colonies on Merritt Island. No one knew how many duskies lived in the St. Johns. In a decade in which the government appropriated billions of dollars for exploring outer space, the Endangered Species Preservation Act was the first official acknowledgment that many forms of life on our own planet faced annihilation.

The dusky became officially endangered in March, 1967—one among a charter group of endangered species that included more than fifty animals in the United States (nearly a half dozen in Florida alone). In addition to the dusky, in Florida there was the closely related Cape Sable seaside sparrow, the Everglades snail kite, the diminutive Key deer, the American alligator, the West Indian manatee, and the Florida panther. Many other species would later be added. Today all but the alligator remain imperiled.

The Endangered Species Preservation Act of 1966 set out a ". . . program in the United States of conserving, protecting, restoring and propagating selected species of native fish and wildlife." The law recognized a range of causes of endangerment, including overexploitation, disease, and predation. Above all else, the law incriminated the loss of habitat. This, of course, was the reason for the dusky's perilous condition. While the law empowered the secretary of the interior to buy land to protect species, it did not prevent federal agencies such as NASA from threatening the recovery of endangered species.

The Tennessee Valley Authority (TVA), for example, continued to destroy innumerable species of aquatic animals in the southeast with hydroelectric dams. A single dam built across the Tennessee River at Alabama's Mussel Shoals in 1924 drove an estimated thirty-five mussel species extinct as well as five of the seven species of river snails endemic to the area—surely ranking among the greatest episodes of federally subsidized extinction in history. By 1967, the nine dams on the Tennessee River had left only twenty-two miles of free-flowing water. In 1975, nearly a decade after the Act, TVA dammed the last free-flowing river in Tennessee, the Duck River, which boasted the greatest diversity of snail species remaining in the Tennessee-Ohio river system. Beyond offering the political legitimacy bestowed by the title "endangered," the 1966 act offered little in the way of concrete protection for the dusky or other endangered animals.

While the Endangered Species Preservation Act was the first law to establish the federal government as the protector of endangered species, its involvement in trying to protect declining wildlife was not new. In 1894 Congress passed the Yellowstone Park Protection Act—after a poacher slaughtered bison in Yellowstone National Park. He had committed no crime, for no laws forbade it.

In 1900 Congress passed the Lacey Act, landmark legislation that greatly strengthened existing state wildlife conservation laws. (On March 24 of that year, a young boy in Pike County, Ohio, had shot and killed what was widely held to be the last passenger pigeon in the wild.) A series of wildlife laws followed the Lacey Act.

In 1901 one of the few remaining eastern Carolina parakeets was taken in Brevard County at Padget Creek. Twelve years later the last known in the wild was shot near Orlando. Meanwhile, a single pair of the birds, Lady Jane and Incus, remained at the Cincinnati Zoo.

Faced with both recent and looming extinctions, by 1913 Congress was considering the Migratory Bird Act, a sweeping law to protect birds. Even as the debate ensued, the last passenger pigeon, a twenty-eight- or twenty-nine-year-old female named Martha, languished in the Cincinnati Zoo, and the following year she died. Her death was followed, in late summer, by Lady Jane's—one of the two remaining Carolina parakeets. About six months later, keepers gathered around the cage to watch the green and yellow body of her mate Incas draw its final breath. And so the eastern Carolina parakeet had also come to an end. With dizzying speed, two of the most abundant birds in North America had become extinct.

The Migratory Bird Act, passed in 1913, declared all migratory game and insectivorous birds "to be within the custody of the protection of the government of the United States." In other words, federal, not state laws, would regulate the hunting of such birds. The government strengthened its hand in 1918 with implementation of the Migratory Bird

Treaty Act with Canada, to protect birds traveling between the two countries. The state of Missouri, feeling that the law infringed on its rights, sued to stop a U.S. game warden, Ray Holland, from enforcing the law. When the case reached the Supreme Court, Justice Oliver Wendell Holmes, writing for the seven-member majority, rebuffed the state and declared that, "Wild birds are not in the possession of anyone. . . . But for the treaty and the statute there soon might be no birds for any powers to deal with."

Numerous laws followed these early ones, including the Migratory Bird Conservation Act of 1929 for federal wildlife refuge acquisition; the Coordination Act of 1934; and the Bald Eagle Protection Act of 1940.

Federal efforts to protect endangered species—or for that matter, to define an endangered species—were formally ushered in with the Endangered Species Preservation Act of 1966. A species was considered "threatened with extinction" if the secretary of the interior determined that ". . . its existence is endangered because its habitat is threatened with destruction, drastic modification, or severe curtailment, or because of overexploitation, disease, predation, or because of other factors, and that its survival requires assistance."

Congress strengthened the 1966 act with the Endangered Species Conservation Act of 1969. The new law charged federal agencies with protecting habitat "insofar as is practicable and consistent with their primary purposes." In other words, still no prohibitions prevented NASA from diking the last habitat of the dusky on the island.

While neither the 1966 nor the 1969 acts prevented destruction of endangered species, their passage in quick succession suggested that the government's license to freely destroy the habitat of endangered species would not last forever. If nothing else, the laws granted standing to otherwise unentitled species; the laws gave conservationists hope that they would at last have laws to fight *with* rather than against.

In March of 1969, Herb Kale—given optimism by the laws but sobered by the rapidly declining fortunes of the sparrow—organized "A Conference on the Ecology and Preservation of the Dusky Seaside Sparrow and its Habitat on Merritt Island and the St. Johns River Marshes, Brevard County, Florida." Ten years after his initial 1954 visit to Merritt Island, Kale had returned to Florida to live, where he became a vocal advocate for the dusky. Like ornithologist Allan Cruickshank, Kale had been drawn to the state by its spectacular bird life. After completing his Ph.D. on the "Bioenergetics and Ecology of the Long-billed Marsh Wren in Georgia Salt Marshes" in 1964 at the University of Georgia, Athens, he moved to Tampa, where he took a job as an ornithologist at the Encephalitis Research Center, a division of the State Board of Health. There he studied the relationship of birds to mosquito-borne viruses. Two years later he began work at the Florida Medical Entomology Laboratory in Vero Beach. Maurice Provost was his boss.

The 1969 conference, held in a room at a Titusville bank, was the first ever on behalf of the sparrow. Kale opened the conference: "Brevard county, Florida, is unique probably in a number of respects," he said to the participants who had gathered. "It is the site of the John F. Kennedy Space Center, a fact known by almost everyone in the world; and it contains the only population on earth of the dusky seaside sparrow, a fact unknown by almost everyone in the world." Kale went on to say that "There is a formula for saving a species from extinction: First, a timely recognition of the endangered species. . . . Then we must do something about it."

In addition to Kale, Jack Salmela and dozens of officials

from various state agencies were there. Representatives attended from the American Ornithologists' Union, National Audubon Society, and The Nature Conservancy. Provost, who had wanted to attend, suffered a heart attack several days before the conference and was recuperating in the intensive care ward of Indian River Hospital. Even though the dusky was still largely unknown outside the county, Kale's campaigning on behalf of the sparrow had brought together an impressive array of ornithologists and officials.

After these opening remarks, a young graduate student in wildlife biology from the University of Wisconsin, who was conducting a study of the dusky, rose to speak. Twenty-four-year-old Brian Sharp had arrived in Brevard County in 1968, and quickly gained a reputation as the dusky's most eloquent advocate. Sharp was articulate and passionate, not the sort of unemotional scientist who spoke only in terms of statistics and probabilities. Born in 1944 in Washington, D.C., Sharp grew up in Thornton, England, a village in Yorkshire, in the midst of Brontë country. His mother was from Philadelphia; and his father was a British naval officer. When Sharp was fourteen, he and his family moved back to Philadelphia; there he won a National Merit Scholarship, entered Wesleyan University in Connecticut, and majored in philosophy, languages, and literature, with a second major in biology. After briefly considering a career in medicine, in 1967 Sharp entered the master's program in wildlife ecology at the University of Wisconsin at Madison.

Sharp explained to the several dozen people gathered at the meeting that he had begun an extensive search of the St. Johns for the dusky, where he estimated there to be almost nine hundred males. He explained that while more sparrows than expected had been found in the St. Johns, the situation on Merritt Island was more critical than ever.

In 1963 Trost had found about seventy pairs of duskies

there. In 1968 Sharp found only thirty-three or thirty-four males. Sharp conducted his census in terms of males because they advertised their presence with song, and the less conspicuous females were difficult to count. Like Trost, Sharp assumed that a female existed for each singing male. In other words, Sharp's census of the thirty-some pairs meant that the population on Merritt Island had fallen by 50 percent in only five years.

The idealistic Sharp had come to Brevard County believing that sound science, straight talk, and a little common sense were all that was needed to save the dusky seaside sparrow. Despite the catastrophic decline, the young biologist held out hope, explaining that the dusky was an adaptable creature and, given half a chance, would survive. What disheartened him most was that, even as the losses rapidly mounted before everyone's eyes, refuge personnel seemed to be in a state of political paralysis.

A few months before he spoke at the conference, Sharp had been walking along a dike by one of the impoundments known as Gator Creek, where he saw a few duskies singing in the broomgrass, when he encountered workmen setting up a pump to flood the impoundment. Sharp immediately went to Curtis Wilson, the refuge manager, and explained what he saw, expecting Wilson to quickly put a stop to it. Instead, Wilson explained that the situation was out of his control. Sharp immediately telephoned Salmela, who was out of the office. At lunchtime Sharp ran into him at a Titusville coffee shop and once again explained what he had seen—how the nesting area of among the last duskies on the island was about to be flooded. The Mosquito Control director agreed to lower the water but refused to keep the impoundment drained. When Salmela asked if this was acceptable, Sharp mumbled, "every little bit helps."

Sharp had been initiated into the politics of the endangered dusky seaside sparrow. Sharp later accused Wilson of "running a duck club" on Merritt Island. Indeed, even Provost had confidentially informed Sharp that "I found Jack [Salmela] more ready to 'yield' on managing for duskies than Curtis!" Sharp described the flooding incident in his field notes, complaining that Salmela ". . . was beginning to call conservationists unreasonable, and that there were some people who just won't be satisfied. . . ."

In addition to providing the first public forum for the conservation of the dusky, several important initiatives stemmed from the 1969 meeting. Most significantly, the Department of the Interior would look into the possible purchase of several thousand acres of prime dusky habitat in the St. Johns. Second, an endangered species biologist would be appointed to the Merritt Island Refuge to work with the dusky. In addition to these important initiatives, there was another that, while impressive on the surface, turned out to be an insight far behind its time: NASA, Mosquito Control, and Fish and Wildlife reached an agreement that would "preserve habitat for the majority of the known refuge population of the endangered dusky seaside sparrow . . ."—a call for instituting essentially what Charles Trost had called for in his study five years earlier. The rising political status of endangered species and the imminent passage of the 1969 Endangered Species Conservation Act now made instituting such a program politically acceptable for Mosquito Control.

The agreement specifically called for installing floodgates in some of the dikes and closing them only during the six-month mosquito breeding season. With the floodgates opened for the other six months, the sparrows and the natural vegetation would have a lengthy reprieve. In theory, mosquitoes could be controlled and the dusky saved—apparently, one without much cost to the other. The agreement called for an extensive study, to run concurrently, to examine exactly what effects the opening of the dikes would have on restoring former dusky habitat.

Unfortunately, the well-intentioned study to "preserve habitat for the majority of the known refuge population of the endangered dusky seaside sparrow" would prove to have less to do with saving the dusky than with preserving—with the exception of one small area—the *status quo* on Merritt Island. And coming as it did just before the expected passage of the 1969 Endangered Species Conservation Act, the study effectively served as a preemptive strike against tightening federal regulations. In other words, the "study" gave the appearance of action while interfering as little as possible with the doings at Mosquito Control.

This study would in many ways duplicate the findings of earlier ones. In 1962, J. A. Kadlec published in the prestigious journal *Ecology* the results of lowering water in "Effects of a drawdown on a waterfowl impoundment"—research closely resembling that of the 1969 study. Trost himself had documented what diking did to the salt marsh: the diking of Merritt Island had reduced the number of duskies by 90 percent. Sharp had documented a 50 percent decline of duskies in the diked area between 1963 and 1968. Furthermore, the plant ecology literature was specific on the consequences of diking: for example, that the broomgrass on Merritt Island, upon which the dusky depended, could withstand up to two and a half months of flooding but no more. In short, an ample body of research already existed upon which to plan a perfectly sound scientific course of action for the dusky.

Nevertheless, the new study was to include three impoundments, consisting of about 1300 acres—2 or 3 percent of the birds' original habitat on the island—where the majority of sparrows on the island lived at the time. These impoundments were known as Black Point, Marsh Bay, and

Gator Creek. In the study originally proposed to Mosquito Control by Fish and Wildlife, Marsh Bay and Black Point would be drained for six months a year, while the dike at Gator Creek would be breached and remain open year-round. Vegetation would be monitored periodically in the impoundments to see if original salt-marsh plants, such as broomgrass, returned.

Salmela went over to Provost's house to discuss the agreement and a short time later wrote to Fish and Wildlife regional director C. Edward Carlson, explaining that *lowering* the water level in Gator Creek Impoundment was one thing, but draining it as the service suggested was ill-advised and a standing invitation to mosquitoes. Gator Creek was directly across the Indian River from town and, if a large brood emerged there, they would probably head straight for "the heart of Titusville." It was the spring of 1969, and with the launch of the *Apollo 11* moon mission only three months away, this was no time for compromise. Salmela reminded Carlson that, in an earlier understanding between NASA, Mosquito Control, and Fish and Wildlife reached back in 1964, the service had agreed not to do anything to hinder mosquito control—and this was a violation of that agreement. Salmela then relayed Provost's suggestion to Fish and Wildlife that it would be better to open up the more distant Marsh Bay Impoundment anyway, because it included more varied habitat than did Gator Creek, so that "the duskies would have the opportunity to show their preference of nesting sites." Salmela supported the idea, but for a different reason: Marsh Bay was the ". . . farthest from populated areas, and if there should be a large brood of mosquitoes, there is a good possibility that the mosquitoes would . . . cause less harm." But the most compelling reason to drain Marsh Bay instead of Gator Creek was not mentioned: nine sparrows lived at Marsh Bay, only five at Gator Creek.

Gator Creek was not the only problem as the director of Mosquito Control saw it. Salmela was also unhappy that the original proposal called for completely draining the other two impoundments, albeit for only part of the year. He suggested that the water be only *lowered* in Gator Creek.

The more northerly Marsh Bay Impoundment would be subdivided by yet another dike; one side would be drained all year, the other half flooded all year. Black Point would be similarly subdiked and managed. On April 11, Carlson sent back a signed agreement with a letter to Salmela, "We have made the changes suggested . . . and believe the agreement is now ready for your signature." Salmela signed the agreement.

On May 5, W. L. Towns, Fish and Wildlife acting regional director, wrote to Salmela that the service, after further consideration, had changed its mind and "would like to amend the dusky seaside sparrow study agreement." After a benumbingly complex series of negotiations, agreements, disagreements, signings, and renegings, a deal was finally reached: Black Point Impoundment, rather than being drained for part of the year as originally stated, would remain flooded year-round for mosquito abatement and thus be used as a "control," or point of compromise. Gator Creek Impoundment would be drained for the dusky for seven months of the year and flooded the other five for mosquito control. Marsh Bay Impoundment would be completely drained.

How did the dusky fare amid this wheeling and dealing? The grand sum of male duskies on the island as the 1969 study commenced was about three dozen—thirty within the three designated study areas and up to a half dozen outside them. Twenty-five lived in the northernmost part of the island—sixteen in Black Point Impoundment and nine at Marsh Bay Impoundment. Five males lived in Gator Creek Impoundment several miles south. Up to a half-dozen duskies, or 15 percent of the island population, lived between the study areas.

The final proposal meant that of the more than 15,000 acres diked on Merritt Island, only about 285 acres within Marsh Bay Impoundment, holding nine duskies, would be drained year-round and returned completely to the sparrow. Another 200 acres at Gator Creek Impoundment would be partially managed for the dusky—that is, opened for part of the year. The two impoundments managed for the partial benefit of the dusky held twenty-one individuals, or 58 percent of the sparrows on the island. So in the end the agreement did seek to "preserve habitat for the majority of the known refuge population of the endangered dusky seaside sparrow." But by a slim majority, indeed.

Regional Director Carlson expressed hope that this "badly needed study [would] halt the decline of the dusky seaside sparrow on Merritt Island Refuge [and] . . . assure permanent recovery of this remnant population." But to no one's surprise, the Fish and Wildlife progress report on the study a year later concluded: "In 1969 thirty singing males were recorded in the study areas, but only seventeen were observed in 1970. This represents a 44 percent reduction in one year." Nearly half the duskies within the study area had been sacrificed to prove a foregone conclusion.

Specifically, Gator Creek had held five birds in 1969, but only two in 1970—and none after 1971. With the sparrows gone, in 1972 Gator Creek was completely flooded for mosquito control. Marsh Bay Impoundment held nine males in 1969, but only one the following year. Only the sixteen sparrows living at Black Point Impoundment fared "well," their population having fallen by only two.

According to minutes of the annual meeting between the U.S. Fish and Wildlife Service and the Brevard County Mosquito Control District held on April 6, 1971, Harold J.

O'Connor, the refuge manager, "was pleased with the recovery of vegetation in [Marsh Bay Impoundment], and said his people were considering various ways of increasing the 'edge effect' by use of burning [and] dynamiting. . . ."

The progress report recommended that the study be ". . . extended an additional two or three years in order to be able to say with some degree of confidence whether or not the management procedures being applied are adequate to accomplish the objective of restoring the habitat of the dusky seaside sparrow. . . . even if the sparrows completely disappear from the refuge, it is felt that this study should continue until enough habitat is restored so that we can attempt to reintroduce individuals onto the refuge from the St. Johns. . . ." Continue the study did, with some modifications. By 1972, only nine duskies were found in the study area. By 1973, only three duskies remained on Merritt Island.

These dealings cut to the heart of the perilous politics of endangered species conservation. Mosquito Control's willingness to debate the issues and compromise at all marked the agreement as a political success. But what was the virtue of political victory when the goal of saving the dusky was lost in the process?

Most troubling, the credible vocabulary of science had been appropriated to mask political motives. A political arrangement came to be known as a "study." And an exercise in lethal research was camouflaged by the words "conservation" and "preservation." Sharp called the arrangement "an abuse of science." It is enough to say that the dusky seaside sparrow was being "studied" to death.

7

The Man on Horseback

Confident and outspoken, Brian Sharp was in many ways Chuck Trost's opposite. Where Trost had been hesitant to rock the boat, Sharp would have happily capsized it—if that's what it took to make his point. Sharp's motto might have come from Edward Abbey: "If saving wilderness is outlawed, only outlaws can save wilderness."

Originally, Sharp's professor, Joseph Hickey, had suggested his student study the rare Ipswich Sparrow, which nested only on Sable Island, off Nova Scotia. But the logistics of the research on Sable were too complicated. Hickey then wrote to Cruickshank. Cruickshank suggested the dusky seaside sparrow. He wrote that the "destruction of the habitat preferred by dusky seaside sparrows has been disastrous to that one specialized species . . . and some fear it eventually may be exterminated."

Captivated by the idea of working with an endangered species and of travel in exotic Florida, Sharp eagerly embraced the recommendation. Working with a small grant secured by Hickey, Brian and his wife Kathi headed for Brevard County.

Like the Trosts, Kathi and Brian Sharp were featured in a local newspaper not long after their arrival. The *Titusville Star-Advocate* heralded their presence in Brevard County as "modern pioneers." When Trost saw a copy of the newspaper, which a friend had sent to him out West, he wrote wistfully to Sharp about how it reminded him of his and his wife's own stay on Merritt Island. In a photograph accompanying the article, Kathi adjusts the strap of Brian's canvas sack, slung at his side as he prepares for a day in the marsh. Binoculars around his neck, he gazes at the ground as if to mentally prepare himself for the rigors of fieldwork. According to the profile, Kathi declared their lives on Merritt Island, where they occupied a small cinderblock house provided by the refuge, "a very simple existence." Her husband corrected her, "Yeah, a kind of lame-brained existence, rather." Like her husband, Kathi was sometimes overwhelmed by the pace of burgeoning Brevard County. Once Kathi drove into town for supplies and got lost in a housing development for half an hour, which pushed her to the edge of tears.

While Trost had spent most of his time on Merritt Island, Sharp, at Cruickshank's urging, turned his attention to the St. Johns. This inaccessible part of Brevard County had remained unknown long after Merritt Island had become a regular stop for birders. A few historical accounts of duskies in the St. Johns were found in the literature. But at the time of Sharp's arrival, no one knew exactly how many birds were still there, or how they were connected historically with the rapidly dwindling Merritt Island population. It is known that during the Pleistocene, the St. Johns River was a brackish lagoon bordered by offshore bars, just as the Indian River is today. Sands shifting southward gradually filled in between these offshore bars, and the waters in the valley began to freshen and drain northward. The valley's prehistoric legacy as a saltwater lagoon had left enough salt in the ground to keep the waters brackish and suitable for the broomgrass and other plants the dusky preferred. The St. Johns was a relic "coastal" salt marsh that existed inland, replete with blue crabs, mullet, and saltwater killifishes, as well as salt-marsh plants and salt-marsh birds. Memories of the land's ancient inheritance are everywhere.

To Sharp, the St. Johns was a poet's river, ancient and meandering in its course through the brackish marshlands, hung in a blue-gray mist by morning, illuminated in copper sunlight by evening—but always bathed in detached and exquisite silence, save for the lonely crying of birds and the murmurs of insects. The St. Johns begins in the marshes of St. Lucie and Indian River counties to the south, but not until Brevard County does a true river channel begin. (The St. Johns and one of its tributaries, the Oklawaha, have the distinction of being the only rivers in Florida to flow north.) Shallow for most of its southern half, the river glides more than flows, tracking a serpentine course across grassy shallows, often only a foot or two deep. After heavy rains, the river fans out into great expanses over a grassy carpet to claim thousands of additional acres.

The river was named by the slave trader Pedro de Quexas, who sailed into its mouth near present-day Jacksonville on St. John's Day in 1519. From de Quexas forward, scarcely a published account exists of a sojourn along the St. Johns in which the traveler does not marvel at the enchanting loveliness of its lushly forested banks. Early French explorers would return to the river time and again to marvel at its wealth of greenery and strange animals such as alligators, egrets, and manatees. In the 1500s René Goulaine de

Laudonnière wrote of the northern part of the river, "The trees were all entwined with cords of vines, bearing grapes in such quantities that their number would be sufficient to render the place habitable. Besides this fertility as a vineyard, one could see large quantities of chinaroot growing round in the bushes . . . the place is so pleasant that it would force the depressed to lift their spirits."

The French explorers met a young native chief who took them to see his father. There they found a "spacious countryside with high pine trees growing close together, and under these we noticed a large number of deer gamboling across the open spaces through which we passed. Then we found a hill side on the edge of a great green valley, and in its open spaces there were the most beautiful prairies in all the world, and the grass was of a good type for pasture. It was surrounded by little freshwater streams and by a tall forest which made the valley very beautiful to see."

In the 1870s American abolitionist and writer Harriet Beecher Stowe, who wintered at a town along the northern reaches of the river, called the St. Johns the "grand water highway through some of the most beautiful portions of Florida." She recounted a river trip in 1872, along two hundred miles of the river on the steamer *Darlington*, commanded by Commodore Rose, a black woman "weighing some two or three hundred pounds, with a brown complexion, and a pleasing face and fine eyes."

The wilderness [was] something quite astonishing. It was the first part of May; and the forests were in that fullness of leafy perfection which they attain in the month of June at the North. But there is a peculiar, vivid brilliancy about the new spring-leaves here, which we never saw anywhere else. It is a brilliancy like some of the new French greens . . . and reminding one of the metallic brightness of birds and insects. In the woods, the cypress is a singular and beautiful feature.

It attains to a great age and immense size. The trunk and branches of an old cypress are smooth and white as ivory, while its light, feathery foliage is of the most dazzling golden-green; and rising, as if often does, amid clumps of dark varnished evergreens—bay and magnolia and myrtle—it has a singular and beautiful effect. The long swaying draperies of the gray moss interpose everywhere their wavering outlines and pearl tints amid the brightness and bloom of the forest, giving to its deep recesses the mystery of grottoes hung with fanciful vegetatiole stalactites.

The palmetto-tree appears in all stages—from its earliest growth, when it looks like a fountain of great, green fan-leaves bursting from earth, to its perfect shapes, when sixty or seventy feet in height, it rears its fan crown high in the air. . . . These scaly trunks are often full of ferns, wild flowers, and vines, which hang in fantastic draperies down their sides, and form leafy and flowery pillars.

One annoyance on board the boat was the constant and pertinacious firing kept up by that class of men who think that the chief end of man is to shoot something. . . . A parcel of hulking fellows sit on the deck of a boat, and pass through the sweetest paradise God ever made, without one idea of its loveliness, one gentle, sympathizing thought of the animals and the happiness with which the Creator has filled these recesses. All the way along is a constant fusillade upon every living thing that shows itself on the bank. Now a bird is hit, and hangs, head downward, with a broken wing; and a coarse laugh choruses the deed. . . . If the object were merely to show the skill of the marksman, why not practice upon inanimate objects? An old log looks much like an alligator: why not practice on an old log? But no: it must be something that enjoys and can suffer; something that loves life, and must lose it.

It was the same year as Stowe's river trip that the dusky seaside sparrow was first described to science, when a naturalist by the name of C. John Maynard, also traveling the popular river by steamer, docked on the south shore of Salt

70

Lake, a few miles northwest of Titusville. Now a shallow, grassy-shored body of water within the labyrinthine waterway, Salt Lake was once deep enough to dock riverboats. Reconnoitering the area by foot on March 18, 1872, Maynard first saw the sparrow and wrote in his journal, "While beating these savannas for rails and gallinules, I was surprised to see what appeared to be a perfectly black finch rise from the ground fifty or sixty yards from me. . . . During the next day my brother-in-law, Mr. Greenwood, brought me a bird which he had shot on the marshes, and which was new to him. I was delighted upon taking it into my hand to perceive that it was similar to the one I had observed the previous day." Before Maynard had officially named the sparrow, Robert Ridgway, an ornithologist at the National Museum, christened it *Ammodramus maritimus nigrescens*. In 1875 when Maynard published his own account of his discovery in the *American Sportsman*, he rebuffed Ridgway for designating the sparrow merely a subspecies, or "variety":

> I am perfectly aware at this time that Mr. Ridgway has already given it a name as a *variety* of [seaside sparrow]. I now, however, as seems to me perfectly justifiable, it being solely a discovery of my own, baptize it a *species*. Allow me, therefore, Mr. Editor, to present to you and the public my new species, *Ammodramus melanoleucus*, the Black and White Shore Finch.

Maynard went on to further dispute Ridgway's claim that the sparrow was only a subspecies, and insisted that it was a distinct species. The competition for the perfect name for the bird, and whether it was a species or subspecies, was the beginning of a century long battle between the "lumpers" and "splitters"—as if the perfect name would somehow enhance or clarify the very existence of a bird. The dusky's scientific name would undergo many revisions. Partly because it was so different from other seaside sparrows and partly because it was so similar, the dusky defied neat classification. Addressing a similar problem over the much debated classification of the giant panda, George B. Schaller commented, "The panda is a panda." So the dusky is a dusky. Maynard's was the only report of the sparrows ever being seen near Salt Lake.

On Merritt Island, Sharp found a mere thirty-three or thirty-four males in 1968. In the inaccessible St. Johns, the birds remained an unknown quantity. All Sharp had to go on were fragmented historical reports of duskies there, and censusing the St. Johns for sparrows would be far more difficult than on Merritt Island. For years the whereabouts of duskies in the St. Johns remained hidden from all but a handful of collectors, who regularly raided dusky nests and sold the eggs to other collectors, universities, or museums. In 1929 Donald Nicholson reported finding about twenty breeding pairs near State Road 50. At the time, Nicholson and local egg collectors knew of at least two other colonies. Collectors tended to pass their secrets from one generation to the next. Collector Joseph C. Howell, Jr. had searched the St. Johns in 1931 and found duskies about seven miles southwest of the Indian River and south of State Road 50. Nicholson found a colony about a mile and a half east of the St. Johns River. Nicholson later came into possession of Howell's notebooks, which described Howell's heretofore secret locations. In 1960, Donald Nicholson wrote elatedly, "Only J. C. Howell, Jr., Wray H. Nicholson and Donald J. Nicholson [Wray's brother] know of these sites!"

Lon Ellis, who has lived on South Merritt Island for more than thirty years, was a friend of Nicholson's and often accompanied him to North Merritt. Curious to find out more about Nicholson, I left Titusville one Sunday morning to visit Ellis. Twelve miles down U.S. 1, I turned eastward at Cocoa and crossed the broad expanse of the Indian River, its surface glistening silver in the sunlight, by way of the Cocoa bridge. I descended the bridge on the south side of the heavily traveled four-lane highway that now cuts across South Merritt. Several hundred yards from the river, I passed a used-car dealership with the lot perimeter demarcated by lines hung with multicolored pennants. That was the spot where, sixty years before, my father had pumped gas at a station owned by his brother-in-law. A Pizza Hut and dozens of fast-food eateries and stores now surround it. Lon Ellis lived only half a mile away, in a small, low house fronted by a spacious screen porch and surrounded by thick palmettos on one side and an orange and lime grove on the other. Ellis offered me a seat, then proclaimed himself a "leaner" due to his disability. I sat down while he took up a station at the end of a freezer on the porch and leaned for the next two hours.

"Egg collecting used to be an admired profession, and people made a lot of money at it. The Nicholson brothers— Don and Wray—had already gotten rich from developing several varieties of fruits, including the succulent Dream Navel orange. After that, they had lots of time to play and to collect eggs. Don had a fiendish appetite for objects. He could have a thousand of the same kind of eggs, but then he'd see one with markings a little different, and he'd have to have that one too. Then he'd have to have a dozen of the new type. By then he'd discovered a new pattern, and so he'd have to have samples of those, too. Egg collectors were the greediest bunch you can imagine. Nicholson was a gritty little bastard, every bit worthy of his trade. He was a short little man. The shorter the height, the bigger the ego. He swore worse than anybody I'd ever heard. Every other word out of his mouth was profanity." Ellis visited Nicholson in Orlando on his deathbed in 1964. Mustering his waning strength, Nicholson told him, "Come over here, you goddamn bastard, so I can get a good look at you!" Several days later the developer of the Dream Navel orange passed away.

The most recent clues Sharp had to go on were from Trost's notes. In 1962 Trost found five dusky pairs along State Road 50, west of Titusville, just where Nicholson had in 1929 revealed a colony of 20 birds.

As he searched the St. Johns for sparrows on foot, Sharp might cover five or six miles a day through the soggy marsh and underbrush. A boat more or less limited one's coverage to waterways. But he found scattered colonies, including a half-dozen singing males a couple of miles southwest of Trost's colony. One day Jack Salmela offered Sharp the use of Mosquito Control's helicopter for surveying the St. Johns. Flying low, one would be able to cover vast areas of marsh, sometimes identifying duskies by their flight as the copter flushed them from hiding. Sharp could then return to these identified areas on foot for a detailed census. Salmela would do just about anything he could to help Sharp find duskies in the St. Johns, for the more found there, the more forgivable would be their loss on Merritt Island.

On May 7, 1968, Sharp climbed into the Mosquito Control helicopter on the tarmac at the Brevard County Mosquito Control headquarters at the airport near Titusville and headed off for an aerial survey of the St. Johns. From the air the marsh resembled a green twill fabric, a landscape with mangrove and palm hammocks stretching to every horizon. Through the bubble of the helicopter, he could see the floodplain of the St. Johns—a wide, flat, wet grassland spotted with ponds. Sharp could see Salt Lake in the distance, as well as Lake Poinsett. After landing once north of State Road 50 to find a small group of duskies still in morning song, he and the pilot took off again and flew south. Minutes later Sharp saw several duskies flush from the grass. As the copter descended, the green landscape resolved itself into meadow flowers, marsh grass, and a cracked oyster shell. Sharp was on the ground again, up to his waist in broomgrass.

He immediately spotted three duskies flying into the tall grass. Sharp waded twenty or thirty yards farther out, then stopped, astounded by the sight: dozens of duskies were flying about. Many of the males were singing. The congregation of duskies was unlike anything he had seen before. With this and subsequent discoveries in the St. Johns, Sharp was finding many times the number that still survived on Merritt Island. It was as if the species were being rediscovered. Several days later, Sharp returned to carefully census the area. Within about three hundred acres of prime dusky habitat, he counted more than a hundred pairs. The dusky, it seemed, had been granted a reprieve.

Sharp wrote to Professor Hickey of a "colony heretofore unknown to the ornithological world." Sharp named it Big Colony. While sometimes escorting reporters and photographers to Merritt Island, Sharp decided not to publicize the location of Big Colony for the time being.

Although still mostly unknown nationally, the dusky's "rediscovery" in the St. Johns heightened the sparrow's profile in the local press. The quotable Sharp always made a compelling case: the sparrow ". . . really puts on a show of bravado . . . [and is] singing away as though he doesn't know he is becoming extinct," he told one reporter.

At the time, a rising chorus from environmental reporters began to condemn Mosquito Control for the extensive destruction of salt marshes throughout Florida. The threatened extinction of the dusky was cited as another case in point of the evils of impoundment. Once a hero, a perplexed Salmela sometimes received letters of condemnation from angry environmentalists. Growing sentiment for the preservation of endangered species and wetlands threatened to turn the world of Mosquito Control upside down.

Initially, the dusky lacked the credentials for national recognition. For years the whooping crane—less than sixty were believed to exist in 1968—had dominated the headlines when it came to endangered species. The "great white bird" possessed a majestic, graceful flight and undertook transcontinental migrations. The dusky was small, nondescript, unmelodic, and rarely ventured more than a few miles. The dusky might have remained largely anonymous but for its association with the Kennedy Space Center, whose fame grew with the Apollo launches.

Sharp realized Mosquito Control's predicament and how the success of his own work on Merritt Island—Salmela's domain—depended on Mosquito Control's cooperation. Thus, an implicit deal was struck. Sharp saw no reason to fan the fires of public sentiment against Salmela; if there was any publicity to be had, "it should be of benefit to the dusky." Sharp assured Hickey in a letter, "In all these dealings with the press, etc., I attempt not to say anything which will cause embarrassment to Mosquito Control."

Sharp's time in Brevard County was a magical time in his life—and his discovery of Big Colony was a high point there. He had made, in ornithological terms, a major discovery, and he had not even begun writing his master's thesis. When a week later he returned to Big Colony on foot, he found a dusky nest "in a bunch of *Spartina*, domed but not quite as much as the nest of a meadowlark, so that the inside of the nest was shaded mostly, although a few speckled pieces of sunlight fell on the eggs, of which there were four, white with reddish brown markings, these thicker toward the heavier end. Some green living *Spartina* was also woven over the top."

On May 28, three weeks after the discovery of Big

Colony, Sharp rented some horses and rode off with Jerome Carrol, the assistant manager of the Merritt Island National Wildlife Refuge, into the St. Johns for a three-day reconnaissance. He had seen the marsh from the air and parts of it from the ground; now he would attempt to cover areas of the St. Johns as no biologist had done before.

He and Carrol set out on horseback near Highway 528, the road to Cocoa, and headed west into the marsh before wending through pine woods interspersed with palmetto. They were soon confronted by the drainage canal that marked the boundary of an impending subdivision of Canaveral Groves, financed by a Miami developer. Following the canal for a while, they finally stopped and had lunch. Sharp was surprised at the extent of the planned housing development, which it turned out lay only a few hundred yards from Big Colony. After lunch, they unloaded the horses and set their gear on an air-mattress. Sharp swam across the canal holding the end of a rope and towing the supplies behind him. Once on the other side he tugged on the rope, attached to the halter of one of the horses, while Carrol, standing on the other bank, pushed them from behind.

That evening, just south of Big Colony in an area of boggy scrub, sweet-smelling shrubs, bayberry, and juncus, they spotted duskies, only to be stalled by a torrential downpour. According to the notes Sharp kept of the sojourn, he and Carrol "took shelter in a tiny hammock. . . . Ate dinner of canned spaghetti and bread, and caught water in the poncho, over a gallon, and filled up our water bags." They were treated to an "evening serenade of duskies. . . . Where we were setting up camp, I was investigated by a barn owl, who was beginning his evening activities. He flew over me twice, and it was still light enough to obtain a nice look. Within five minutes, walking through a few palm trees, I flushed a screech owl, who landed a little ways away on the broken-leafed trunk of a sable palm, allowing me to approach within a few feet of him before he flew again. Jerome lost one of the food bags containing all the matches, so we went to bed without a fire."

Next morning they mounted and cantered onto an abandoned road, where Sharp got stung on the hand by a colonial wasp. The day would be one of the most memorable of his life. The trace rambled through a riparian wonderland—what Sharp would later describe as "a salt grass meadow, dotted with marsh pinks and bespeckled with golden coreopsis, dotted with palm trees stretching lime-green to the far horizon." They emerged at one of the highest points in all of the St. Johns—the map called it Possum Bluff—fifteen feet above sea level. It lay within a half mile of Big Colony. Entanglements of broomgrass reached waist-high, and duskies flew about. To Sharp, Possum Bluff was one of those Deep South dreamy places like the Suwannee River, with its live oaks hung with Spanish moss, "my vision of the Elysian fields, or the most magical place on earth."

The three-day journey by horseback through the St. Johns covered some of the best remaining subtropical wilderness in Florida. Although the water table of the St. Johns had begun to recede at the edges, Sharp could still write of the area: ". . . some of the country we rode through was exquisite, looked quite virginal in fact, ungrazed, unburned, unditched, trackless, a gentle grassland dotted with palm trees, almost intoxicating, riding in the morning sun. I suppose these past three days will prove to have been the high point of my sojourn here. No newspapers, no cars, no cops, only the slow creaking of leather and the steadiness of the horses."

After reconnoitering Big Colony on horseback, Sharp spent the next several months censusing the St. Johns—on foot or bicycle where the land was dry and flat. Though nowhere were the birds so extensive as at Big Colony, he

found other nesting colonies several miles north, on eithe side of State Road 50. By the time Sharp had finished h census that spring, he estimated that there were 984 males and about as many females—throughout the St. Johns (i cluding the more than 100 in Big Colony).

Few people were more elated about the discovery of E Colony than Jack Salmela. Not only was he genuinely hap for the sparrow, but this also gave Mosquito Control an c should the birds totally disappear from Merritt Islar Salmela was once quoted by a newspaper reporter, "] would hate to be the cause of any species becoming extin In his more generous moods, Sharp acknowledged t "Salmela always expressed concern about the dusky." Sharp remained deeply troubled over the declining fortu of the birds on Merritt Island, whatever new hope was ad by the St. Johns discovery. Sharp felt that Salmela dragged his feet when it came to the dusky and made token modifications of the dikes. He thought Salme "tyrant who would stop at nothing to meet the town fatl antimosquito agenda." Sharp also saw Salmela as an "en of the dusky—and by extension, as his enemy. Sharp w later resent Mosquito Control's claiming credit for the covery of Big Colony since the helicopter had been ir mental. This, along with Provost having commissioned to do the first study of birds on Merritt Island, would su that Mosquito Control was dedicated to ensuring the di survival.

More than once Salmela reminded Sharp of Mos Control's contributions. After reading Sharp's thes 1968, Salmela wrote to him: "I wish you would give c consideration to your comment, 'But the best interests dusky have up to now been ignored.' If the Florida Board of Health and the U.S. Fish and Wildlife Servi not been concerned, [Trost's] work would not have bec

reality. Dr. Provost and the Bureau deserve a great deal of credit for initiating this study."

In a lengthy and otherwise pleasant critique of Sharp's thesis, Provost also took him to task for the same statement: "I was even . . . trying to get funds to investigate the effects of impounding on birds, especially on the dusky. Without this there would have been no Trost paper in Bent's series to refer to—although the latter does not acknowledge either the [Fish and Wildlife] contract, us, or the very considerable assistance given Trost by Jack Salmela and the Brevard County Mosquito Control District."

To Sharp, Mosquito Control's claims for studying the duskies' decline was a little like "a tobacco company claiming credit for generating a lot of knowledge on lung cancer." After discovering Big Colony, Sharp lamented, "Borrowing that helicopter was a big mistake. It was as if Salmela owned a part of my soul."

Salmela, with a wary eye to history, carefully documented his disagreements with Sharp. He even catalogued newspaper articles in files at his office and carefully annotated any of them that might cast Mosquito Control in a bad light. Attached to a wire-service story, "Rarer than Whoopers," in which Sharp was quoted, the hypervigilant Salmela wrote a note, as if to address his own posterity: "Sharp was reluctant to search the St. Johns for duskies. He already had a sensational article prepared for publication condemning Mosquito Control for extirpating the dusky. He only consented after I offered the use of our helicopter. . . ." Actually, Sharp had already begun to search the St. Johns on foot. And he hadn't "prepared" the piece but had been heavily quoted in it, claiming that the dusky was in eminent danger of extinction, and laying the blame at Jack Salmela's doorstep: Mosquito Control ". . . should have thought of [the dusky] when they were first planning the dikes"; and, "They'd hate to have an

extinction on their record." Then came the unexpected discovery of Big Colony—and what seemed a reprieve for the dusky. Salmela felt that this cast Sharp as a scaremonger, for the new data had changed the picture considerably. The dusky wasn't "rarer than whoopers" after all. Salmela was under the impression that the article would therefore not be published. In fact, the article apparently was already in press at the time of Big Colony's discovery because it came out in *Science News* two weeks later. Published or not, Salmela wasn't about to let such an occasion go undocumented.

Salmela had no kind words for the reporter either. As the Mosquito Control director wrote to Provost, "I wonder if he is aware of the fact that you instigated the study to learn the plight of the duskies, or if he even cares? I suppose we will have to learn to live with this sort of thing."

8

Road to Nowhere

The year following Sharp's discovery of Big Colony, the Florida State Department of Transportation announced plans for a four-lane highway right through it. The Martin Anderson Beeline Expressway would extend an existing road from Orlando in Orange County, cross the river at Possum Bluff, then head straight to the town of Cocoa and to the east coast. A separate fork would be built north from the main line to Titusville.

When Assistant State Highway Engineer Curran J. Schenck for the first time publicly revealed plans for the highway at the 1969 Titusville dusky conference, Kale, Sharp, and others attending were incredulous. Joseph Hickey, who was also there, exclaimed that "the new Beeline plan was a stunner. It will go smack through the best dusky area."

When Kale pressed Schenck on the particulars of the

highway and its effect on the dusky, Schenck explained that numerous animals had become extinct in the past and would continue to do so, and he questioned the wisdom of wasting money to try to save a bird of such little consequence. Officials of the Expressway Authority, which would manage the new toll road, believed that the dusky was smart enough to move elsewhere—a belief seconded by Fish and Wildlife's Vero Beach office. Besides, Schenck said, if tourists were to enjoy the pristine beauty of the St. Johns, they would need a road through it.

Looking toward the future, Sharp wrote of the project, "What is the point of transporting huge numbers of people . . . in the 1980s if the unique Florida countryside is raped, subdivided, industrialized, and unrecognizable?" Sharp was particularly concerned that the roadbed would act as a long dike across the marsh and affect water levels. Schenck assured him that the state road department would minimize the impact of the roadbeds on the marshes.

Kale, like Sharp, was also concerned that the roadbed would eliminate the natural flow of water essential to the broomgrass's survival. As he wrote to an acquaintance, "The Beeline extension is fouling up the area west of the St. Johns, natural drainage is being badly blocked, even the main channel of the river has been filled in. If this is an example of what will occur when they get east of the St. Johns then they are going to hear screams from here to Washington and back."

Kale angrily questioned the need for a new highway. Brevard County was already a tic-tac-toe board of cement and asphalt roads. U.S. 1 and Interstate 95, then under construction, ran north-south through the county. Three other highways ran east-west between Orlando and Brevard County. These highways, running nearly parallel, were only a few miles apart—and lightly traveled. Not only did the county commissioners want to build another highway, they would send a branch of it north toward Titusville. Worse yet, the road would be located right smack in the middle of Big Colony.

In November 1969 the Florida Department of Transportation applied for a federal permit for a bridge across the St. Johns. Sharp was asked to comment on the proposal. He wrote that the highway threatened perhaps one-fifth of all duskies in existence and that this stretch of the river was "one of the wildest and most exquisite areas in the whole of the St. Johns River Valley headwaters. The aesthetic effect of high-speed traffic on the environment is, by its very nature, negative. I suspect that the *mere presence* of the expressway will have an adverse effect on the surrounding marsh. . . . I really cannot say what will happen over the years to the marsh which is enclosed between the proposed highway fork. I, like Dr. Kale, question the need for such a forked highway in order to be able to save a few minutes driving time."

By early 1971, permits were in hand and bonds had been sold to finance the highway. Hal Scott, executive director of the Florida Audubon Society, in a letter to H. A. Solberg of the U.S. Coast Guard, which issued permits for structures over navigable waterways, faulted the Department of Transportation's environmental impact statement because it did "not emphasize the threat to the endangered dusky seaside sparrow. . . . According to the research of Mr. Brian Sharp, the habitat is much more extensive than what you have indicated. . . . Are we to risk the loss of a species just because the 'bonds are sold' for a road? We are certain that travelers will be happy to drive a few extra miles out of their way in order to save a whole species."

The Florida Audubon Society then proposed an elegantly

simple plan for completely by-passing the dusky area: simply widen the existing roads between Orlando and Brevard County rather than build a new one. Kale then offered yet another alternative. He argued that the main highway should be built, but without the separate routes to Titusville and to Cocoa. This might at least spare some of Big Colony. Kale reminded planners that only a few miles east of the proposed fork to Titusville and Cocoa, I-95 could have interchanges to both these cities. Let Beeline motorists to Titusville or Cocoa exit at the interstate. But Schenck told Kale there had to be a fork with separate routes to these cities because the Beeline would pass over I-95 without any interchanges to it. The presence of I-95 was therefore irrelevant.

After several token changes, like moving the bridge site three hundred yards, highway construction began. Sharp visited the marsh and likened it to "a scene from Dante's Inferno." One day in 1970 Kale happened to drive by the construction site. Interchanges were, in fact, being built between the Beeline and the interstate. By then it was too late to prevent a separate feeder route through the vicinity of Big Colony.

In the end, Big Colony was strangled by highways. The Cocoa branch of the Beeline skirted the south edge of the nesting grounds, while the feeder route to Titusville ripped into its northwestern flank. I-95 bounded it to the east. Big Colony had been reduced to a triangular island of broomgrass marshland, surrounded by major highways.

Unfortunately, problems for the duskies did not end there. At the urging of Fish and Wildlife, the highway department had earlier agreed to modify its plan for placing a borrow pit for fill dirt directly in the midst of Big Colony. The department of transportation agreed to obtain fill elsewhere. The department then ignored the agreement and dug a twelve-acre pit at the original site, obliterating five nesting territories. Today this water-filled pit sits atop what was the last large breeding area the dusky would ever know.

The Beeline Expressway in Brevard County had a far more contentious and complicated history than Kale or Sharp could ever have imagined. Long before plans for the road had become public, local politicians had been haggling for months over the highway's proposed route. Ultimately, the highway's course was dictated not by need but by political clout and insider dealing. The state road department had originally planned for the highway to cross the river at Possum Bluff and continue east—without a fork to Titusville and Cocoa but connecting with I-95. Titusville-bound motorists could indeed exit at I-95 and take the highway north. Cocoa-bound motorists could drive south. This was exactly the alternative path for which Kale would later argue. But if this course made sense from an economic and conservation point of view, it didn't make sense politically—at least to the Brevard County commissioners, for this course did not grant adequate importance to the presence of Titusville and the Kennedy Space Center. As far as the commissioners were concerned, having a major road in the county that did not directly link the space center through Titusville would have been like the Appian Way bypassing Rome. When the county commissioners first heard of the Beeline extension and how its course threatened to virtually ignore the space center, they were incensed.

Lee Wenner headed the county commissioners at the time. A Brevard County native, Wenner served as chairman for eleven years, in addition to six as vice-chairman—much of it during runaway development of the county. Years earlier Wenner had served as director of Mosquito Control and had actually appointed Jack Salmela as his replacement. Wenner believed that the commissioners in neighboring Orange County had selfishly dictated the original course of the highway to get people from Brevard County to Disney World near Orlando, or to allow people visiting Orlando quick access to the beautiful beaches of Brevard. Wenner felt that if Orange County was to reap the rewards of Brevard County, then Brevard County should benefit from Orange County. This could be done by drawing people from Orlando to the Kennedy Space Center—Brevard's biggest attraction—by building a direct, easy highway connection with the space center. And so the idea of a connector road north was born. Unlike Interstate 95, the fork north would provide a "direct link" with the space center. The Brevard County commissioners vowed to block the Beeline's entry into the county until the Orange County commissioners agreed to build a fork from the Beeline directly to Titusville and the space center. The extension didn't make sense in terms of traffic demand, for ample roads already connected Orlando and Titusville, and these were lightly traveled. But the Beeline fork would look good on a tourist map: the new, conspicuous highway was meant to bolster the town's image and vacation trade.

This Orlando–space center link was but a fragment of a grand scheme of the commissioners. Not only would Brevard County dictate the eastern course of the highway; it would even demand control over the course of the western end in Orange County as a price for entering into Brevard. At the time of the proposed extension, the Beeline began at the Orlando International Airport. The Brevard County commissioners wanted it immediately extended westward to Disney World. Brevard County and the Kennedy Space Center could then reap some of the millions of tourists that came to visit the fantasy land. As Titusville Congressman Lou Frey told a local reporter at the time, "It is important that the Beeline be completed prior to the opening of Walt Disney World."

According to the county, the completed highway would also ". . . serve as a direct defense highway between the missile complex and defense plants located in the Orlando area." NASA had evoked national security on Merritt Island as justification for the indiscriminate diking of the marshes. Now, a few miles away, the dusky had again become a threat to national security. How could an insignificant sparrow hold such sway over a nation?

9

Cities in the St. Johns

As the Beeline was being built through Big Colony, General Development Corporation and other speculators from Miami were buying up most of land between the forks of the future highway. Speculators knew that this land just west of the space center and about midway between the communities of Cocoa and Titusville was a swamp with a future. Several miles from the nearest towns, the land was still cheap. In time, Titusville and Cocoa would grow toward the development. Residents of the future settlements of Port St. Johns and Canaveral Groves wouldn't have to drive to a city; cities would come to them.

Draglines worked around the clock beneath lights on reinforced steel cabs to cut miles of canals to drain the land. Bulldozers transformed the area more in one day than had a millennia of hurricanes. Surveyors with their hard hats and transits partitioned the land into invisible parcels for ownership. Soon would come the buyers.

The entire infrastructure of the future community—sewers, water, and electricity—would be installed. But at the density of houses planned, local wells and septic tanks would be inadequate. One person's septic field would foul another's well. Only by hooking into the central sewer system and water supply from Cocoa five miles away could the developments be established. To nurse the developments along, in 1968 the county commissioners and the developers entered into a complicated agreement. The first one-third of the "settlers" on any given block would rely on individual wells and septic tanks. Once the one-third mark had been exceeded, General Development Corporation agreed to underwrite the cost of connecting that part of the development to the city water supply—lest one person's faucet spout the wastes of another's toilet. Finally, when houses covered two-thirds of each block, the developers would provide central sewage lines to the houses on that block. As long as such arrangements were profitable, General Development Corporation kept its promise to home builders. But after the cost of building the central sewer and water supplies exceeded the profit from selling lots and building homes, the company abandoned the development, leaving homeowners stranded for adequate services—and leaving the city of Cocoa to foot much of the $1.5 million bill for completing the systems. For the next two decades the company enacted similar scams throughout the state and, in the mid-1980s, filed for bankruptcy, with several of its officials pleading guilty to fraud.

The Brevard County commissioners had been no match for the developers that descended on Brevard County during the space boom. Natives were unaccustomed to the fast money and payoffs that had long become part of the fabric of the sprawling communities of Dade County farther south. Even the county fathers proved to be easy prey to schemes. More often than not the developers left crippled communities in their wake. No sooner had Brevard County awoke from its long slumber as a backwater, wide-eyed at the prospect of its becoming a center of the space age, then it realized that it had been robbed of the best of its future. A land that had once astounded visitors with its wildness would have some tourists departing with a new bumper sticker: I Survived Brevard County.

As the General Development Corporation settlement of Port St. Johns took root, the Dubbins brothers from Dade County were buying up many hundreds of acres of marsh two miles south, also within the fork of the Beeline. This would become the county's newest community, Canaveral Groves. The brothers hoped to bypass some of the zoning laws and building codes that a wiser Brevard County was finally beginning to impose on developers. County laws, for example, stipulated that developers register their plats with the board of county commissioners and obtain approval directly from the board. In an attempt to make an end run around these restrictions, the Dubbins registered their development plan with the county circuit court instead of the commissioners. Once some roads had been built, the brothers showed up in County Commissioner Wenner's Titusville office with a proposal: they would give him a valuable parcel of land if the county would maintain the roads—even though the roads had not been approved by the commissioners and fell below acceptable standards. Wenner told the "bastards to get the hell out of town." A few days later a third brother, a judge in Dade County, came before Wenner to plead his brothers' case. Wenner gave him the same instructions.

But the brothers had already established an elaborate scheme to defraud buyers at Canaveral Groves. They produced a prospectus, distributed nationwide, with maps and photographs showing roads throughout the development. It portrayed Canaveral Groves as an idyllic landscape along the space coast, and the land was offered at bargain prices. Many people bought the land sight unseen, making a fifty-dollar down payment through the mail and monthly payments thereafter. When a would-be owner retired and showed up to see his land, he usually could not find it. There were, in fact, no roads leading there—and if there had been, they would have been submerged for much of the year. The furious buyer's first stop was usually the county commissioner's office.

"You probably own land somewhere out there, but you'll need an airboat to get to it," Wenner would tell them. The owners would stop payment, and the developers would foreclose, then resell the land to the next victim. Some property was sold three and four times. This land, much of it at the heart of dusky habitat, was changing hands so fast that no one knew who owned it.

Many of the county commissioners themselves grew rich speculating in Brevard County real estate during the boom years by purchasing land they knew was slated for development. When I-95 was first proposed through the county, one of the road board members gave the county commissioners a map of the proposed route. Two commissioners bought land where interchanges were going to be. One of them later became a judge. Such insider dealing was not illegal, but ethically questionable.

Other commissioners, such as Wenner, grew wiser but neither richer nor more powerful. He cared deeply about the future of the county and grew to detest the developers. But even for Wenner conservation had its limits, for he believed in "saving whales and eagles and all our wildlife, but when you have one type among a hundred species, like the dusky, it's not all that important."

So the sparrow's numbers continued to decline. In 1968—before the construction of the Beeline or the completion of the developments—Sharp had counted more than 100 pairs in the area of the proposed forks. With the expressway and the developments complete, by 1977 only a dozen pairs remained there. And within the St. Johns as a whole, the nearly 1000 pairs Sharp had estimated in 1968 had been reduced to a handful. Today the rare person living in the developments of Canaveral Groves or Port St. Johns—which now encroach on the area once occupied by Big Colony—has ever heard of the dusky seaside sparrow.

10

Brevard County Revisited

One afternoon in 1990 while in Brevard County, I drove down U.S. 1 toward Port St. Johns. Just before the Video Food Mart, I turned west onto Fay Boulevard, the main road through the development. I drove for a mile or two past a tightly packed grid of house-lined streets. After crossing the I-95 overpass, I made a right onto Homestead Avenue, then a left onto Corsica Boulevard. Several blocks down Corsica, I intersected Aberdeen Avenue, which bordered the edge of the site where Big Colony had once thrived. Comfortable homes now lined the street. It was trash day; plastic garbage containers and heaps of junk were stacked on the curbs. A large discarded wood-framed poster depicting "Space Travelers" was propped against a trash can. Rows of photographs, grouped according to space mission, depicted crews from the early Apollo launches to the *Challenger* disaster in January 1986. I wanted to take the print as a piece of memorabilia of the place and time—the space program and Big Colony. Through the break in the palmettos and cabbage palms farther down the avenue, I could see the low, golden marsh, the floodplain of the St. Johns, and the area where Big Colony had thrived fifteen years ago. I parked my rented car at the end of the street and stepped out. Two children ran in a nearby yard, tossing a red speed ring. One young boy made repeated attempts to catch it in a baseball glove.

At the end of the street—which still lacked houses—I walked a few feet into the marsh, or what remained of it. The ground was dry, even though it was the rainy season. I saw little evidence of broomgrass. A wide drainage canal lined by a barrier of woody shrubs stood at the back of the development. I walked past a trash pit containing the twisted aquamarine remains of a molded plastic kiddie pool. A half-dozen empty cement bags lay flattened in the black soil.

I walked farther along the street. Just past the intersection of Aberdeen and Corsica, at the edge of the development, stood an aluminum gate posted with a Fish and Wildlife sign emblazoned with the profile of a flying Canada goose: Unauthorized Personnel Prohibited. This marked the boundary of the Beeline Tract of the St. Johns National Wildlife Refuge, which had been set aside for the dusky. Bordering the refuge stood a house with a swimming pool beneath a modern screened dome. A woman with long dark hair hauled herself from the water and perched like a gargoyle on the tile drain at poolside. At night, bathroom lights shine into the edge of what was once Big Colony.

I continued walking through the neighborhood. A young couple was tying a black tarpaulin over their boat, docked on a trailer in the yard. "Looking for anyone in particular?" they called. I told them no. We chatted for a while. Neither had heard of the dusky, and they seemed surprised when I told them it once had lived only a couple of blocks away. The husband's face betrayed his worries; his wife said he was about to lose his job at Martin Marietta. "We'll sell our boat and move right back to Long Island," she said definitively.

On my way out of the subdivision, I stopped by the local library and asked the librarian if there were any newspaper clippings or other materials on the history of the development.

"When did it begin?" she asked.

"Late sixties and early seventies," I told her.

"That's not history; it's modern times!" she declared. "We have nothing."

As I walked back to the car, a slate bank of clouds moved in. By the time I was behind the steering wheel, big flat gray pellets of rain were striking the windshield. Wind gusts turned the trees inside out. Waiting for the storm to subside, I sat in the car listening to the local news: the Discovery shuttle mission had been postponed because of a hydrogen leak, and the recently launched billion-dollar Hubble Telescope was found to have blurred vision. I turned off the radio. A few moments later the rain stopped. The sky gradually blued. Beyond the last row of houses, steam genies rose from the distant marsh by the river. A marsh hawk climbed a spiral staircase into the sky. I watched until the bird was out of sight, then drove back toward U.S. 1, lowering the visor against the sunlight splintering through the windshield. But for the puddles and a few storm-tossed palm fronds on the pavement, the world had returned to normal; and in its own strange, persevering way, seemed as perfect as it could ever be.

11

Refuge

U rged by the Florida Audubon Society and other state conservation groups and bolstered by funds allocated under the Endangered Species Conservation Act, in 1969 the U.S. Fish and Wildlife Service first seriously considered establishing a refuge for the dusky in the St. Johns. This would be the first refuge ever for a songbird. Several sites were originally considered. The site of Big Colony would have been an obvious choice—had developers not beaten Fish and Wildlife to the land. The only other feasible site was along the northern side of State Road 50, about seven miles north of the future Beeline, where Sharp had found a sizable number of sparrows. This so-called north-of-50 site was, indeed, the last best hope for the dusky. Commercial developments had not yet made inroads into the area, although a small section of sixty-five acres had been set aside for an women's orphanage, the Hacienda Girls' Ranch.

Once the land had come under consideration by Fish and

Wildlife, Paul Sykes, Jr., a service biologist with the Endangered Wildlife Research Program, went out to survey the property. He found that a long dike with a road on top had recently been built from State Road 50 north for about a mile and a half toward the Hacienda site. As he reported, "This causeway and ditch cuts right through the second largest concentration of duskies." Just south of the highway, a dragline was digging ditches, piling spoil in a continuous line eight to ten feet high alongside the canal. Realizing that these two canals were bleeding dry the best of what little dusky habitat still remained, Sykes wrote to C. Russell Mason, executive director of the Florida Audubon Society: "It now becomes readily apparent that if something is not done, and done in the very near future, to establish a sanctuary or refuge on the St. Johns, the habitat of the dusky seaside sparrow will be destroyed or rendered unsuitable for the species in that area. It is frightening to see how rapidly this area is being transformed."

After much deliberation, late in 1969 Fish and Wildlife asked its Land Acquisition Review Committee (LARC) to consider buying land for the dusky seaside sparrow. The bureaucratic machinery creaked into motion. Realty, the branch of the Fish and Wildlife responsible for land acquisition, requested a "biological and engineering study." Following the preliminary reports, the acting regional supervisor, division of refuges, wrote to the regional director, ". . . this is one example of land acquisition that could mean the difference between survival and extinction of a species. . . . We recommend another meeting of the Land Acquisition Review Committee as soon as possible." LARC tentatively approved buying land north of State Road 50—contingent upon working out an agreement with the Army Corps of Engineers on maintaining desirable water levels. Fish and Wildlife then submitted the proposal and a letter of intent to purchase to the director of the Florida Game and Fresh Water Fish Commission, requesting concurrence from the state. The proposal and a letter explaining the current status of the dusky was also sent to the Bureau of Reclamation. After a flurry of correspondence between Washington, Atlanta, and the local office, in April 1970 the director of LARC recommended the acquisition of 3595 acres of dusky habitat north of State Road 50 with money provided under the Endangered Species Conservation Act. But Fish and Wildlife still had to obtain the required permits and approvals. First, the State Planning and Development Clearinghouse had to be notified of the acquisition. Then the assistant secretary of the interior had to assure the chairman of the Council on Environmental Quality, Russell E. Train, that the proposal to establish the St. Johns National Wildlife Refuge would be in accordance with the requirements of section 102 of the National Environmental Policy Act of 1969. Miles of red tape were processed, tens of thousands of dollars were spent, but not a square foot of land was bought for the dusky.

At the dusky conference held in Titusville in 1969, Terry Blunt, eastern regional director of The Nature Conservancy, had told Russell Mason that the conservancy itself would buy the all-important initial piece of land north of State Road 50 for the refuge. This would not only discourage potential development in the area; it would energize Fish and Wildlife's lethargic efforts. Mason inexplicably rejected the offer, although perhaps he felt that Florida Audubon, as premier protector of the state's wildlife, should not have to rely on an outside group. Instead of moving ahead with the refuge, at the conclusion of the conference Mason appointed a temporary working committee that would appoint a permanent committee to study the problem.

Karl F. Eichhorn, Jr., one of the members of the commit-tee, as well as president of the Indian River Audubon Soci-ety, a charter member of the Florida Audubon Society, was growing impatient with the slow progress of the refuge. He declared the idea of Mason's committee a fiasco and wrote to Blunt: ". . . Florida Audubon Society has not responded to the challenge to save the dusky. Action is urgently needed now." In other words, the conservancy's offer was needed.

Eichhorn sent a copy of his letter to Kale, who re-sponded, "I am in agreement with your comments about the inadequate effort of FAS to do something about the dusky. I had planned to raise hell about it. . . . The loss of this species is going to rest on the heads of all of us in Florida."

Eichhorn also carbon-copied his letter to Fish and Wildlife in Atlanta. The acting regional director at the time, W. L. Towns, assured Eichhorn in a letter of June 12, 1970, "we have sufficient control here . . . we do not see the need for action by The Nature Conservancy." Towns explained that there was no rush to purchase land because "the real es-tate market in Brevard County is such—at this time—that we see no possibility of developmental changes before we can move with our acquisition program." It was a baffling re-sponse, given that Atlantic Capes Investment Corporation of Miami had bought 3200 acres on the opposite side of the highway only a few months before and was laying plans to drain the land for development. Four months after Towns' letter of reassurance, land in the heart of the proposed refuge suddenly went up for sale. Having misread the situa-tion, Fish and Wildlife was caught by surprise, and still with-out funding, sent an urgent plea to The Nature Conser-vancy. Within three hours The Nature Conservancy had bought sixty-three strategically located acres just north of State Road 50, effectively forestalling further development in the area. It was the kernel around which the St. Johns National Wildlife Refuge was established the following year. Fish and Wildlife later bought the land from The Nature Conservancy, then added another 4100 acres. The dusky, it seemed, had found at last a safe haven from human encroachment.

12

Wildfires

At the turn of the century the heath hen, once common throughout much of New England, had been reduced to only a few hundred birds, all living in a federal refuge on the island of Martha's Vineyard, Massachusetts. In the summer of 1916 a brushfire burned the heart of the refuge, killing all but a handful of the birds. The last reported sighting of the heath hen, a race of prairie chicken, was on March 11, 1932. Years later the Department of the Interior, which managed the refuge, evoked the experience to point out the ever-present danger of fire to a species in a limited habitat.

Like the heath hen, the last duskies were also confined to a small fire-prone refuge. By the 1970s, an ominous pattern of burnings scorched the St. Johns National Wildlife Refuge. Even though technically a dusky refuge, the land continued to be "managed" as it had always been—not for the sparrow but for surrounding ranchers and landowners. The Hacienda ditch that Sykes had earlier reported remained open, draining the refuge. The land grew dryer, with the broomgrass yielding to woody vegetation. Even as neighboring ranchers routinely set fires in the winter dry season to increase pasture forage for cattle in spring, Fish and Wildlife failed to cut fire lanes around the refuge.

On March 21, 1974, a wildfire—begun by ranchers burning neighboring land—was driven by forty-mile-per-hour gusts through 1900 acres of the refuge, burning much of the habitat the refuge was meant to protect. Censuses conducted later in the spring showed a loss of at least twenty birds in the burned areas. The following winter, another wildfire devastated much of the refuge. In fact, between 1970 and 1977, six different wildfires swept through parts of the refuge, leaving fewer duskies each time. Most likely the duskies escaped to inhospitable habitat, where they were apparently eaten by predators. In any case, very few escapees could be accounted for. By 1975 only forty-seven males were counted in the St. Johns Refuge; two remained on Merritt Island. With the duskies pinned in so small an area, fire had become among their biggest threat.

Ironically, fires had always played a role in shaping the marshes where the dusky lived. Fires kept the grass low and the nesting areas prime. But these were natural summer fires, ignited by lightning, and they were quickly doused by the showers that invariably followed. Nature ignited and extinguished its own fires. In addition, ponds and other large wet areas of the marshes served as natural firebreaks. But no rainstorms came to extinguish the "controlled burns" set by cattle ranchers in the dry winter season. Match-lit conflagrations often scorched thousands of acres. These fires also exhausted much of the life in their path, for they burned harder, hotter, farther, and longer than nature had ever intended—or than the dusky or its habitat could repeatedly endure.

With fire jeopardizing the duskies to the north of State Road 50, in 1974 Refuge Manager Robert Yoder sent a memo to Kenneth Black, Fish and Wildlife regional director in Atlanta, recommending acquisition of an additional 1120 acres—but not north of State Road 50. As a precaution, he suggested buying what little land remained in the vicinity of Big Colony. The best of the land there had been swallowed up by development; but given the imperiled state of the dusky, every acre seemed vital.

Herb Kale, meanwhile, repeatedly warned the Atlanta regional office about the threat of fire to the refuge. He and others urged that machinery be bought to clear fire lanes around the refuge. In September 1975, after repeated unanswered requests for equipment, Yoder wrote a six-page plea to Black explaining the critical need for fire equipment by November, when the winter fire hazards would start. "[Fire] is considered a principal factor in the 60 percent decline in dusky population between 1972 and 1974. The time frame on acquisition of this equipment is somewhat critical," Yoder wrote. Three months later the regional office still had not responded.

On December 28, 1975, a rancher used torches to start fires on his own property just north of the refuge. A sudden cold front that afternoon stirred powerful southwesterly winds that pushed the fire through the western half of the refuge, burning nearly 2100 acres. The fire then jumped the ditch along the north boundary of the refuge and continued scorching key habitat. Thirty-six male duskies had been seen in this area the spring before; only seven survived the fire. One sparrow escaped into a small unburned patch of broomgrass. Beau Sauselein, a biologist at the wildlife refuge, reported that six others had flown across State Road 50. Not long afterward, the area immediately south of the state road was burned by its owner. No duskies were ever seen there again.

Still there was no response from Atlanta. Two months later two more wildfires burned on the refuge. One started near State Road 50 and burned approximately 400 acres. The other fire began at the northeast corner of the refuge along I-95 and burned about 550 acres. Four males and two females had been seen there the previous spring. The areas burned by these fires included the best dusky habitat on the refuge.

With probably less than three dozen males remaining in all of the St. Johns, in 1976 the service began buying land in a panic for what would become known as the Beeline Tract. The St. Johns National Wildlife Refuge had sprung up in two discontinuous, widely separated areas of the marsh. Realizing that the initial Beeline purchase would not be enough, Fish and Wildlife later bought land left over from the large tract of land owned by General Development Corporation.

Kale was livid about the fires and wrote to Hal Scott, president of the Florida Audubon Society: ". . . the paperwork for the fire lanes languished on desks in Atlanta (over a year and a half or more!). But, Merritt Island National Wildlife Refuge personnel sure spent a lot of time on duck management on Merritt Island (first things first, of course!)." Then he wrote a letter to Nathaniel P. Reed, assistant secretary of the interior, lambasting Fish and Wildlife for the two-year delay in constructing the fire lanes and adding:

> If the Fish and Wildlife Service had prepared the fire lanes that were recommended over two years ago, the fires started by ranchers to the north would not have moved onto the refuge. . . . This refuge was purchased specifically in an ef-

fort to prevent the dusky seaside sparrow from becoming extinct. That lack of a concerted management effort on the part of the Fish and Wildlife Service . . . is inexcusable. The dusky seaside sparrow and the St. Johns National Wildlife Refuge should not be relegated the status of a part-time side project to be worked on willy-nilly by Merritt Island National Wildlife Refuge personnel."

Kale's better judgment caused him to first send the letter to Hal Scott, "in the event that you may not think it should be sent on FAS letterhead. If it does not meet with your approval, let me know and I'll send it on plain stationery." Scott sent it on the Audubon Society letterhead, but only after expunging a paragraph charging, "Considerably more effort is being given to managing Merritt Island National Wildlife Refuge to enable duck hunters to shoot species that are nowhere near as endangered as is the dusky seaside sparrow."

The dusky population in the north-of-50 part of the refuge had plummeted: The 143 males Sharp had counted there in 1970 had dropped to 110 by the spring of 1972. By the following year only 54 males remained, and by the spring of 1974, only 37 survived. By the spring of 1976, there were 11 males on the northern part of the refuge—and only 28 in the entire St. Johns.

In March of 1976, Kale received a conciliatory letter from Assistant Secretary Reed, stating that Fish and Wildlife could "understand and appreciate your concern over the recent wildfire." A few weeks later, Lynn Greenwalt, director of the Fish and Wildlife Service in Washington, D.C., wrote to Scott: "I assure you that the U.S. Fish and Wildlife Service has a total commitment to restoration of the dusky."

In 1979 the refuge reported, "At the present time we have a complete system of fire lanes. The danger from wildfire has been greatly reduced through prescribed burning and the development of this fire lane network." By then, no more than nine males survived on the northern part of the refuge—and only two dozen in all the St. Johns. Not a single female had been seen since 1977.

13

Collusion

Throughout the daily calamities and momentary reprieves that marked the history of the dusky, the sparrow's fortunes, in a larger sense, continued to rise and fall with the vicissitudes of federal endangered species legislation in Washington. The Endangered Species Preservation Act of 1966 had given the sparrow political status; the Endangered Species Conservation Act of 1969 had, among other things, eventually granted it land for a refuge. If these early acts had marked the legislative awakening of the environmental movement, the Endangered Species Act of 1973 marked the passage into what many conservationists believed to be an age of enlightenment. Michael J. Bean of the Environmental Defense Fund, in Washington, called the law "A determined attempt to keep the concept of the biblical ark afloat."

The 1973 act not only made it easier to buy land for endangered species, but refined and expanded the definitions of earlier acts. For the first time the law distinguished among degrees of rarity: *Endangered* applied to ". . . any species which is in danger of extinction throughout all or a significant portion of its range." *Threatened* meant ". . . any species which is likely to become an endangered species within the foreseeable future." Furthermore, the 1973 act extended protection not only to species but to subspecies and to distinct populations of either.

One of the most powerful and controversial provisions of the 1973 act, known as section 7, explicitly forbade federal agencies from jeopardizing the continued existence of endangered species and stated that "*all* Federal departments and agencies shall seek to conserve endangered species and threatened species and shall utilize their authorities in furtherance of the purposes of this Act." The law also prohibited any federal agency from destroying "critical habitat," or land required for an endangered species to survive and recover. These prohibitions applied not only to federal activities, but also to any federal permits or agreements that might harm endangered species. As federal agencies, NASA and Fish and Wildlife clearly were bound by the law.

The legal strength of section 7 of the 1973 act had been strictly interpreted in a landmark case concerning another federal agency, the Tennessee Valley Authority. A ruling by the U.S. Court of Appeals for the Sixth Circuit—later upheld by the Supreme Court—prevented the closing of the floodgates on the recently completed the $109 million Tellico Dam in Tennessee because it threatened an endangered subspecies of fish. The case was officially known as TVA v. Hill, but was more popularly known as Tellico Dam v. the snail darter, or people v. fish.

Prior to the 1973 act, Fish and Wildlife could legally bow to the wishes of Mosquito Control and NASA, regardless of the impact of diking and other activities upon the endangered dusky. In fact, this collaboration stemmed back to

1964, soon after NASA ceded the huge buffer zone around the space center to Fish and Wildlife to manage as a wildlife refuge. Fearing that the land might be allowed to revert to mosquitoes, NASA required Fish and Wildlife to sign an agreement to manage the land as to "neither interfere with the District's mosquito control program, nor create or prolong conditions that favor mosquito production." Through the agreement, Fish and Wildlife in effect ceded control, and while ostensibly managing the area as a wildlife refuge, Salmela, at the behest of NASA, actually managed it for Mosquito Control. (The two schemes were compatible as far as ducks went.) Several years later, with the impending passage of the 1969 Act, Fish and Wildlife apparently grew uneasy with the 1964 concordat, and in a new agreement agreed to refrain from management activities that would "pose too great a potential mosquito problem"—the interpretation of which would rest with Mosquito Control. The shading of the agreement had changed; the substance had not. Mosquito Control still ruled Merritt Island, endangered species and all. Fish and Wildlife's status had been raised from that of a peon to a supplicant. The 1969 agreement broke no law; it merely violated the spirit of Fish and Wildlife's obligation to endangered species.

Section 7 of the 1973 act, however, cast very serious doubt on Fish and Wildlife's prior agreements with NASA and Mosquito Control. Yet the service continued to collude in the flooding of dusky habitat. By that time, however, any allegation of the service contributing to the extinction of the dusky seaside sparrow on Merritt Island was rapidly becoming a moot point, for only two of the sparrows remained there.

Under the 1973 act, even the dusky's extirpation from Merritt Island would not have relieved Fish and Wildlife of the responsibility to protect remaining "critical habitat" at Marsh Bay, Black Point, and elsewhere on the island. As long as the duskies remained, there or in the St. Johns, the law required protection of any land designated as essential to the bird's recovery.

Perhaps sensing the sweeping prohibitions that would come with the 1973 act, in 1972 Mosquito Control removed the subdike across Marsh Bay. The following year, although the dike had begun to be removed from around Black Point—a task that wouldn't be completed for another six years—parts of the impoundment continued to be flooded. On February 5, 1976, Refuge Manager Yoder wrote to Salmela that this impoundment ". . . was at one time inhabited by dusky seaside sparrows and has potential for future dusky use." Yoder explained that "This potential will be enhanced if the impoundment is drawn down." On April 27, Yoder again wrote to Salmela, specifically requesting that the water be *lowered* that summer. In his letter Yoder explained that two duskies recently had been spotted in the impoundment. Two months later, Mosquito Control complied. While concessions were made in that the water was lowered, this critical habitat continued to be more or less flooded.

In 1977 Stephen R. Vehrs became refuge manager and soon began questioning the service's failure to enforce the 1973 Endangered Species Act. On August 11, 1978, Vehrs requested an opinion from Regional Solicitor Raymond C. Coulter in Atlanta "concerning our responsibilities and jurisdiction over mosquito control activities on the refuge." More than a year later, during which time critical habitat continued to be flooded, he still had not received a reply. In June, 1979, the refuge decided to implement still tougher restrictions for managing the dusky. Recommendation Four, for example, called for the *complete* draining of Black Point, at least for part of the year. The usually accommodating Salmela balked at this, however. He knew that particular impoundment was a "breeder," and if allowed to revert to natural marsh, could play host to major seasonal mosquito outbreaks. Vehrs, meanwhile, still waiting for a reply to his original inquiry to the regional solicitor, complained in a letter to Regional Director Black, "We have had difficulty in getting compliance from the Brevard Mosquito Control District in the implementation of Recommendation Four. Recommendation implementation is beginning to become difficult." Vehrs was reluctant to push the issue of Black Point with Mosquito Control without a legal opinion behind him, fearing that breaking Fish and Wildlife's prior agreement with Mosquito Control might prompt NASA to take back refuge land, totally removing it from the jurisdiction of the service. Of course, whether NASA or Fish and Wildlife managed the land was irrelevant in terms of endangered species law: the sparrow still had to be protected. While an opinion such as Vehrs requested would normally be turned around within a month or two, this was one nobody seemed eager to dig into. Not until nearly two years after Vehrs' original request did Coulter finally respond in a letter to Black. His response was unequivocal:

> Section 7 of the Endangered Species Act of 1973 . . . requires federal agencies to insure that any actions they fund, authorize or carry out do not 'jeopardize the continued existence' of any endangered or threatened species or destroy or adversely modify the critical habitat of such species. This mandate, which applies to the Fish and Wildlife, as well as NASA and other federal agencies, has no mitigating language. . . . [The] Act prohibits the Fish and Wildlife Service and NASA from authorizing the continuation of such practices.

According to the Solicitor, only extraordinary conditions would allow a federal agency to escape the stringent requirements of the 1973 act, and then, exemption could be obtained only from a special Endangered Species Review Board. In 1990 I wrote to Fish and Wildlife's regional office in Atlanta to see if such an exemption had been obtained. A month later I received a reply: "We are not aware of any exemption being granted to the U.S. Fish and Wildlife Service, NASA or the Brevard Mosquito Control District."

The solicitor's opinion confirmed what some people within Fish and Wildlife had silently suspected all along: ever since 1973 the service had been violating the Endangered Species Act by colluding in destroying dusky habitat. It seemed that nothing less than the sparrow's extinction could put Fish and Wildlife's malversations on legal ground. Then "critical habitat" would no longer be designated, for nothing would be left to protect.

Provost, meanwhile, had been sidelined by health problems, leaving Salmela to face a rising storm of criticism more or less alone. Nor would Provost have to endure the political and ecological aftermath of diking, the dusky's disappearance from Merritt Island, or its decline in the St. Johns. In making decisions for the sake of the county's immediate mosquito-control needs, he committed future generations to a course of action. But while he and others would witness the immediate benefits of his decisions, the subsequent complications would outlive him. After a series of heart attacks stretching over nearly a decade, on December 1, 1977, Provost complained to his wife that he was tired; he lay down on the living room couch and died. Two weeks later a dusky seaside sparrow was spotted for the last time on Merritt Island.

14

Recovery Team

Shortly after the passage of the 1973 act, Fish and Wildlife established the practice of appointing a recovery team for each endangered species. According to the service, "Recovery teams will . . . consist of on-the-ground professionals who carry the greatest responsibilities and expertise with respect to the animal concerned. . . . it is imperative that team members and leaders be selected with utmost care."

Among other things, these teams would plan conservation strategies. By 1975 a team of experts had been assembled to chart a course to save the dusky seaside sparrow. Jim Baker, the refuge biologist since 1973, was appointed team leader.

Baker had begun his career with the service in 1968 as a seasonal employee at the Noxubee Wildlife Refuge in eastern Mississippi. It was there—at Bluff Lake—that he met his future wife Gail, whom he married that same year. Baker received his Ph.D. in waterfowl ecology from Mississippi State University in 1971. His thesis was on the ecology of wood ducks. An expert in ducks, it was understandable if Baker knew nothing about the dusky seaside sparrow when he first came to Merritt Island. Upon learning of his appointment in 1973 as steward of the refuge where the famous sparrow lived, Baker went to tell an ornithology professor and friend at Mississippi State, Jerome Jackson.

According to Jackson, "Baker came to me ecstatic, 'I've just got a job as a Fish and Wildlife biologist to study the dusky seaside sparrow! What is the dusky like? Is it anything like a house sparrow?'"

Jackson felt that "It was a case of Fish and Wildlife hiring someone who knew absolutely nothing about the sparrow. There was a qualified biologist who had actually done his thesis on the dusky who couldn't get a job in biology because Baker had been appointed to the position. Baker was a good man and friend of mine. But he was a victim of the 'good old boy' system—the same system that ultimately victimized the dusky."

Also appointed to the team was the omnipresent Herb Kale. By this time, Kale had begun to devote much of his time to the dusky; he brought unmatched enthusiasm and knowledge to the team. Paul Sykes, the endangered species biologist with Fish and Wildlife, was hired as a special consultant.

Also on the team was a reluctant Lovett Williams, director of the wildlife research laboratory of the Florida Game and Fresh Water Fish Commission in Gainesville. Williams pleaded with his superiors at Fish and Game not to put him on the team because, as he told them, "I don't know anything about the dusky. It's inappropriate. I have nothing to contribute." While the recovery team appointment guidelines took professional affiliation into consideration,

Williams knew that his appointment was contrary to the spirit of the idea. His participation had nothing to do with "utmost care" that Fish and Wildlife stipulated. For that matter, his appointment did not necessarily have anything to do with saving an endangered species. His was a political appointment. But Williams' boss wanted the Commission to be represented, and so he instructed Williams to accept Fish and Wildlife's appointment.

Sharp, the leading authority on the dusky, had not even been seriously considered as a team member. Indeed, Sharp was the well-qualified ornithologist mentioned by Jackson who had earlier had been overlooked for the job of refuge biologist. At the time, Sharp worked at the Bird Banding Laboratory at the service's Patuxent Wildlife Research Center in Maryland. Several months after Baker's appointment as biologist, Earl Baysinger, Sharp's boss at Patuxent, attended a Fish and Wildlife meeting in Atlanta. Baysinger was told about how Sharp and his wife Kathi had once been caught skinny-dipping on Merritt Island. Was that the kind of employee Fish and Wildlife wanted? Within the service, Sharp was seen as a risk. Baysinger, who later amusedly related the whole story to Sharp, learned that after the skinny-dipping incident, Sharp's credentials as real Fish and Wildlife Service material in "refuges" were pretty much gone. Sharp was rankled but not surprised that he was not asked to be on the team. The welfare of the dusky was incidental to the politics of appointment. No amount of expertise could compensate for the fact that Sharp did not fit into the system; he was not a good old boy. And unlike most of his colleagues, he did not like to hunt, casting him even further outside the mainstream.

Sharp's philosophical, ethically centered view of conservation continued to brand him as a lone wolf within the service. While his colleagues might be concerned with the dusky's decline, Sharp was profoundly disturbed by it. He once wrote to Kale, contemplating the formidable task of saving the sparrow and the compelling reasons for trying to do so:

> I often stop to consider with a certain amount of wondering incredulousness the necessity of doing something like this consciously. Incredulously, perhaps because doubting the adequacy of the human consciousness to act divinely. But the potentiality of it is fantastically exhilarating. To perform an act of grace, based first on human knowledge, limited as it is, but more importantly, based upon more than this. It is the justification that is intriguing . . . justification usually consists either of poetry or economics, but here I am searching for an enlarged definition of reason. Acts of grace are to be thought of in human terms, in terms of what is humanly satisfying, in fact enhance the human condition. It seems that dignity is of utmost importance—to be dignified. Not self-righteousness, but a dignity acquired through actions, in particular acts of graciousness and, therefore, beauty."

Sharp's was a sad and unjustified fate: the career of one of Fish and Wildlife's most dedicated biologists had been cut short by political ideologues. After several years at Patuxent, the twice-burned Sharp was transferred to the Portland, Oregon regional office, where he continued his disenchanted career with Fish and Wildlife. His explosive temperament surfaced more often as his frustration over his career—and his marriage—grew. After ten years together, he and Kathi separated and divorced. Several years later, in 1990, after twenty years in Fish and Wildife, Sharp, "by mutual agreement" with his superiors, resigned.

To Sharp, Baker epitomized Fish and Wildlife's own shortcomings—philosophically and otherwise. In particular, Baker embodied the service's preoccupation with waterfowl. But even Baker recognized that the service's obsession with ducks was killing the dusky. "I resent that," he once told a reporter. "I'm crazy about waterfowl. But it's an over-simplification to [argue] that we've improved the habitat for ducks when, on the other hand, we blew it for the dusky."

Fish and Wildlife failed to understand the influence of its own history on its endangered species management practices. The service's priorities had been cast in the 1920s, when its ancestral agency, the Bureau of Biological Survey, began pouring its resources into stemming the drastic decline in waterfowl populations during the Dust Bowl. With the passage of the Migratory Bird Conservation Act in 1929, Congress authorized the purchase of private lands for migratory bird refuges. Thus, with ducks in mind, the national refuge system was created, as well as the first concerted effort by the government to protect the nation's wetlands.

In 1939 the Bureau of Biological Survey was transferred to the Department of the Interior and merged, in 1949, with the Bureau of Fisheries. From this hybridized union came the United States Fish and Wildlife Service. While the central office would remain in Washington, the agency's jurisdiction would be divided among seven regional offices throughout the United States. These regions were further divvied up into area offices.

Regardless of locations, waterfowl remained at the core of this new agency's policy. A Canada goose was for a time the service's official mascot, emblazoning everything from uniforms to stationery. Not until later did legislation expand the list of species protected by refuges to include all forms of endangered animals and plants. But a number of upper-echelon employees—many of whom had begun with the service as duck enthusiasts—would formulate Fish and Wildlife policy in later years, when endangered species such as the dusky, not ducks, became the pressing problem. To them, protecting a species such as the dusky was an afterthought.

Sharp complained that management of the dusky was fatally colored by the service's ". . . duck mind-set. A beautiful new refuge like Merritt Island comes along, and all they know how to do is to manage it for goddamn ducks. If Fish and Wildlife seemed to follow instincts rather than reason, this was partly the reason why."

Baker philosophically belonged to the old guard. Sharp criticized him for spending too much time on ducks, among other things: "Every so often I called Baker from Oregon and asked him how things were going with the dusky. 'Oh, just fine,' Baker would say. The fact is that during the four years Baker headed the recovery team, the dusky seaside sparrow went virtually extinct."

While unprepared for his role in trying to save the dusky, almost everyone who knew Baker described him as a kind and joyful man. He loved Beethoven and Mozart and Bavarian polka music—tastes his wife attributed to his German heritage. Baker also loved to eat and to drink white wine and beer. He sported a beard, stood six-feet four-inches tall, weighed 230 pounds, boasted a pot belly and a cholesterol count of 305. An avid hunter, Baker shot so many ducks that he was partially deaf in his right ear. He was nicknamed Big Gizz—an allusion to the thousands of duck gizzards he had cut open looking for lead shot in the course of studies of lead's effect on waterfowl. He and his wife often fished for speckled trout in the Indian River. They'd quit when one of them—usually Jim—caught twenty-one. In 1973 he won the *Field & Stream* sixty-third annual fishing contest for open salt water by catching a large sea trout. The mount, now hanging on the wall of the refuge headquarters on Merritt Island, is accompanied by a framed certificate:

> This is to certify that James L. Baker, Titusville, Florida, on
> the date inscribed below, did hook and successfully land a

sea trout which has been weighed and measured true to record thereof duly entered in the official register of the Field & Stream Annual Fish Contest.

January 31, 1973
12 pounds, 8 ounces
2 feet   9 7/8 inches

Two years after its formation, the team produced a dusky seaside sparrow recovery plan fifteen pages long. Fish and Wildlife then took another two years to review and approve it. Four pages summarized what was already known of the dusky (based principally on the research of Trost and Sharp); one page contained a map of the dusky's range; and one page contained a bibliography. The remaining nine pages presented, in three different formats (flowchart, list, and narrative), twenty-two recommendations—most of which were painfully obvious: ". . . maintain and develop existing and selected potential habitat; restore and maintain optimum population [of duskies] on newly developed and existing habitat; develop public awareness of the dusky and its habitat needs by disseminating information to the public; and monitor population levels by periodic surveys." There were a few specific recommendations in the proposal, among them what particular parcels of land should be purchased for protection or how particular parcels of habitat must be managed.

Raised in the fire-as-management-tool school of ecology, Baker underestimated the importance of water to the dusky's survival. While the report laid plans for controlled burning, the dusky was dying because canals continued to lower the water table and reduce periodic flooding. The plan totally neglected the history of destructive water management in the St. Johns. The Upper Basin Diversion Project, for example, orchestrated by the Army Corps of Engineers over the last century, had narrowed the floodplain of the entire St. Johns, which once stretched nearly twenty miles wide throughout the river's course along the western edge of Brevard County. Rain, instead of swelling the river, drained out of the St. Johns through the Melbourne-Tillman drainage ditch and into the Indian River. Along the eighteen miles of river between Lake Poinsett and Ft. Pierce, the once ample plain was reduced to scarcely two miles wide, with citrus groves and pasture usurping the reclaimed land. This, more directly than fire, hastened the decline of the dusky in the St. Johns. The central facts in the decline of the dusky in the river valley had been completely ignored by the recovery plan, even though it took four years to finalize.

On completion of the plan, the recovery team dutifully made its recommendations to superiors in Atlanta and Washington. Fish and Wildlife approved the plan, then shelved it. The team got a glowing letter from the Atlanta regional office for "doing a fine job."

The birds had vanished totally from Merritt Island. Only a half dozen remained in the St. Johns.

15

The Decision

Purchasing of land for the dusky continued and would soon total an impressive 6200 acres, for which Fish and Wildlife had paid $2.6 million. With word out that the government was buying up prime dusky habitat in the St. Johns, one owner began "improving" his land by burning it over to convert it from cheap dusky habitat into more valuable pasture. Although the land would be rendered almost useless for the sparrow, the "improved" land commanded a higher market value, and Fish and Wildlife would have to pay more for it. The service would then have to turn around and "improve" the land for the dusky—a costly task for which time had long since expired.

Another owner in the vicinity of Big Colony agreed to sell his land to Fish and Wildlife only if the service agreed to take off his hands another tract of inaccessible—and therefore unsaleable property—on the other side of the Beeline. Because no duskies happened to live in the unsaleable parcel (although it was good habitat) Fish and Wildlife refused. If the owner had agreed to sell the dusky tract alone, Fish and Wildlife theoretically could have plugged the drainage canals on the land to restore the original habitat for the dusky. But it could not legally plug the canals because that would have flooded the right-of-way to the other privately owned tract of land. What little chance the dusky might still have to survive therefore rested with the acquisition of the inaccessible parcel of land, for without it, the inhabited tract would continue to be drained.

On August 31, 1978, staffers gathered in the Atlanta regional office to consider the fate of the dusky seaside sparrow. Land already bought was mismanaged. And why spend more money on a bird when no females were known to exist? Had not the sparrow already slipped into the realm of the living dead?

Discussions about the dusky were being conducted against a larger national debate about endangered species in general—an acrid imbroglio that questioned the entire foundation of the 1973 act following the court decision that had abruptly halted the expensive Tellico Dam project.

Attorney General Griffin B. Bell, dressed in traditional swallow-tailed morning coat for the occasion, personally argued the government's case to have the ruling overturned. But on June 15, 1978, the U.S. Supreme Court upheld by a six-to-three vote the decision to bar opening of the dam. This fanned the fires against the act.

Endangered species legislation had become a topic of frequent ridicule in Congress. New Jersey congresswoman Helen Meyner expressed mocking concern for imaginary endangered birds such as the "ruffled spouse" and the "double-breasted seersucker." In testimony before the Senate Environment Committee, Donald C. Simpson of the Pacific Legal Foundation, a prodevelopment group, referred to the White

House's longstanding rodent problem, saying that "after 20 years of interbreeding in an isolated location such as [the executive mansion], it is possible that unique subspecies or lower taxa have developed for which the White House is a critical habitat. Should not the extermination of these unique mice be enjoined?" Against this cynical backdrop, staffers gathered in Atlanta to chart the future of the dusky seaside sparrow.

Not surprisingly, the decision reached by the regional office was in keeping with the political winds from Washington. On September 5, Regional Director Black sent a memo to the Washington office, recommending that, "We hold the line on future land acquisition." Black suggested using the several million dollars that would be saved for ". . . reprogramming to high priority land needs for the American crocodile," in Key Largo. He also suggested putting some of the money into a movie as well as news releases, "to tell the story of the dusky and its final status." The story was never told—a wise move by Fish and Wildlife from a public relations point of view.

Kale and others were dismayed and angered by the decision to abandon any attempt to purchase the vital piece of land. Warren B. King, of the International Council on Bird Preservation, wrote to the director of Fish and Wildlife in Washington:

> We believe that the Service has fallen down in its efforts on behalf of this subspecies. We recognize the Service has limited funds to carry out its work. . . . On the other hand we see no justification for a reduction in effort by the Service at what is probably the most critical time in the existence of this sparrow.

By amending the 1973 act in November, an overwhelming majority of Congress voted to weaken the protections afforded to endangered species. While not affecting the endangered status of the nearly extinct dusky, the new law caused the withdrawal of nearly 2000 pending species-listing proposals because compliance with the new procedures under the amendment proved impossible to meet. The heyday of endangered species legislation in the United States seemed to have passed as quickly as it had arrived. If the 1978 amendment had set back the act, the Reagan administration two years later would effectively cripple it.

The truth was, many Brevard County residents were relieved to see the expanding refuge and efforts on behalf of the dusky halted. They saw their tax dollars being squandered on the land and on "welfare" for a bird that many of them had never even seen. Their sentiments sometimes were inflamed by the press, as some reporters began riding the wave of antagonism against endangered species legislation. An article in the *Sentinel Star* cited a statistic from Brevard County Property Appraiser Clark Maxwell: removal of the 6000 acres comprising the two units of the refuge from the tax roll caused the county to lose $37,000 annually. Although the Federal Government reimbursed the county for $20,000 of this total each year, Maxwell reminded people that "this reimbursement is from tax money." The land could have been easily developed for ranchers, greatly increasing tax revenues for the county. As the article explained, "Maxwell said that land, which is closed to the public to protect the delicate habitat of the sparrow, could readily be developed for grazing 'by digging a few canals.'"

16

Last Gasp

F or almost a quarter of a century—ever since Rubert
Longstreet's warning in 1955—there was talk of the
dusky seaside sparrow becoming extinct. Committees were
established to ruminate over the possibility, meetings held to
talk about it, studies conducted to measure it, and strategies
implemented to avert it. But it was as if all this activity had
occurred behind a veil of denial. Few people seemed to grasp
the raw truth: the dusky's imminent extinction was not a
theory but a piercing reality. And most people, having
buried the reality beneath well-intentioned studies and still-
born committees, suddenly saw the truth come bursting out,
and they seemed to panic.

In 1979 the Florida Game and Fresh Water Fish Commission declared an emergency meeting in Gainesville, and it
convened within months of the tenth anniversary of the first
conference held on behalf of the dusky in Titusville, in
1969. Authorities on the dusky were urgently summoned to

commission headquarters in Gainesville. Even Sharp received an invitation from the state to attend. Charles Trost, who hadn't been back to Merritt Island in years, flew in from Idaho. Kale, Baker and his assistant, Beau Sauselein, Endangered Species Biologist Paul Sykes, and Refuge Manager Steve Vehrs were there. And once the participants had been brought together, organizers did about the only thing they could: call for another furious round of studies to "prevent the immediate extinction of the dusky seaside sparrow." In particular, the studies would set out to determine the factors behind the sparrow's slide toward extinction.

After almost twenty years of intensive studies that had begun with Trost in 1962, there was no question about what was killing the dusky. DDT had reduced the early population, Mosquito Control had finished the job of eliminating the sparrows from Merritt Island, and a major expressway, two large housing developments, draining of the marshes, and a series of wildfires had all but killed them off in the St. Johns.

Specifically, over the course of three days, the emergency committee proposed nine different studies on how to save the dusky, at a total cost of $141,000. When Sharp was given an outline of the proposals, he let go with furious marginalia. Next to the statement "The ecological conditions to which the dusky had adapted are not well understood," he wrote "Bullshit." Sharp, whose 1968 thesis was on the ecology and management of the dusky seaside sparrow, knew more than anyone about the dusky's ecology. He had cited numerous studies on the ecological requirements of salt-marsh plants, which described the vegetation in detail. The new proposal nebulously alluded to the possibility of a "breakthrough discovery" to manage the dusky. "No," Sharp scribbled. He felt that the time for fantasy had passed. Another proposal read, "Determine differences and similarities in behavior among the subspecies of the seaside sparrow that might contain a clue to the peculiar vulnerability of the dusky seaside sparrow as compared to the others." To this Sharp responded: "This is a copout—dusky can do fine if habitat provided." And in response to a proposed "flock [of duskies] at the lab" Sharp wrote, "Seaside sparrows don't 'flock.'"

The emergency meeting also hoped to lay groundwork for a captive breeding program for the dusky, in which the survivors could be taken into aviaries. The emergency program even called for studying a seaside species closely related to the dusky, since it was presumably too late to study the dusky itself.

For the life of him, Sharp could not understand all of this. Earlier he had gone out into the St. Johns marsh. He saw no duskies that day. As he walked along the Hacienda Road, he was amazed to find that the huge ditch along side it was still bleeding water from the refuge. Sharp had understood from a telephone conversation with Baker months earlier that the ditch had already been plugged.

"What's this fucking ditch still doing here? This has to be plugged! Here we are, managing an endangered species refuge for the red-winged blackbird, one of the most common birds in the U.S.," he muttered. Not until June 26, 1979, almost a decade after the land had been bought for the dusky, was the Hacienda ditch finally plugged.

Sharp was utterly bewildered. And he wasn't the only one. Warren B. King had written to Lynn Greenwalt, director of the Fish and Wildlife Service in Washington to complain, "Why has this canal not been plugged?" Why had it taken Fish and Wildlife ten years to accomplish a job that a laborer with a pick and shovel could have completed in a single afternoon? Baker had told Kale that a county commissioner who owned land in the area told the refuge manager not to fill it in, for this would have raised the water table, increasing the risk of flooding. The commissioners, not Fish and Wildlife, ran Brevard County.

Before the meetings ended, Trost and Sharp spent a couple of hours together flying over the land they knew so well—in Jack Salmela's helicopter. Up to that moment, both Sharp and Trost clung to the slim hope that another dusky nesting area might be found in the vastness of the St. Johns. High above the marshes, their strained optimism collapsed. They both knew the dusky was gone.

When Trost got back to Idaho, he wrote a report on his trip and sent it to the participants. He accused some people of actually plotting to eliminate the dusky—a group of "selfish hominids" in the area who had much to gain by development. Ranchers wanted to eliminate the sparrow from the marshy areas suitable for grazing their cattle. The general public demanded complete mosquito control and better duck hunting. Wrote Trost:

> Any way you look at it, the dusky stands in the way of progress. At the risk of being called paranoid, I'd like to describe a scenario of events. . . . Perhaps a county commissioner or some other such powerful local person has seen just how thoroughly Endangered Species legislation can shut down the system. He is dedicated to progress in Brevard County and many of his, and his friends' investments may be in jeopardy. Perhaps we are naive to think that a study such as [Sharp's] wouldn't be useful in the wrong hands. A person could learn precisely where to put ditches in order to do the most damage to a pest species.

Conceding that his accusations might be far-fetched, Trost was nonetheless helpless to explain several "enigmatic" events—including Fish and Wildlife's refusal to fill the canals on its own refuge:

> I find this hard to believe, and wonder what sort of prior

agreements were made to allow this. What in the devil are cows doing grazing the last remaining dusky habitat?

Trost concluded that "outright lies" were told about certain drainage canals in the St. Johns. As always, there was a note of regret in Trost's tone. He lamented that if only the emergency meeting had taken place five years before, there might have been time:

> The condition now looks so desperate that there really isn't much choice of what to do. . . . I don't think it can be overstated how grave the situation really is. It may be that we are too late with too little.

A few weeks after returning home, both Trost and Sharp received thank you notes from the Game and Fresh Water fish Commission for attending the meeting. "We think that the spirit of goodwill generated at the meeting will aid us in our common concern, to give the dusky every chance to continue in its natural habitat." Never mind that the overwhelming consensus of the participants was that the sparrow was already doomed in the wild.

17

The Last Wild Dusky

On July 23, 1980, Herb Kale, Beau Sauselein, and Bill Leenhouts, who had since replaced Jim Baker as chief biologist for the dusky refuge, waded into the broomgrass a mile from the Beeline Expressway, searching for a lone dusky that had been spotted there on several earlier occasions. Aluminum Green, as the elusive sparrow came to be known, had been captured and equipped with two bands in 1978—a numbered aluminum one and a green one—and released. By 1980 he was the sole survivor of Sharp's Big Colony—the last sparrow to have withstood the assault of the Beeline Expressway and the housing developments through his habitat.

By late 1979 only four sparrows remained in the St. Johns, and the whereabouts of each was more or less known. One male known as Orange Band lived alone on the refuge north of State Road 50. He was named after the plastic orange band that had been fitted on him two years earlier, on July 25, 1978. Usually he was known as just Orange. He also

131

wore an aluminum band stamped with the number 1011-41278. Two unbanded males lived on private property just south of State Road 50. With little left to do but watch these individuals die, in 1980 Fish and Wildlife granted the Florida Game and Fresh Water Fish Commission a permit to capture the survivors, holding them in captivity while biologists continued to search for females.

As Leenhouts waded through the broomgrass only a few hundred yards from the spreading destruction at Port St. Johns, he wore a hard hat with a small speaker strapped to the front. The speaker wire ran to a small cassette tape recorder in his pocket. The taped song of a dusky burst intermittently from the speaker. As the sparrows dwindled, the task of randomly flushing a single bird from the grass grew more difficult. Tape recorders, like hundreds of other items such as computers and cameras, had been included on Fish and Wildlife's list of restricted goods. Purchasing one required a six-month process of review and requisition. Leenhouts could not wait that long, so he and Baker went out and bought the fifty-dollar recorder and passed it off as "electronic components," circumventing the labyrinthine procurement procedures.

When they spotted the sparrow in the marsh, singing from a tall stiff stalk of broomgrass, Leenhouts, Kale, and Sauselein draped three forty-foot-long gossamer mist nets across the marsh in the fork of the Beeline, then circled behind the bird. "If he flies toward you, flap your arms and make some noise to keep him going toward the net," Leenhouts instructed. Slowly they walked through the grass, hooting and hollering. Soon, a small sparrow lifted from the broomgrass, arched forward in the dusky's characteristic fashion, and ended up tangled in the net. Leenhouts let out a whoop and dashed through the grass toward the struggling bird. Kale, meanwhile, stepped up and slowly untangled it, expecting to find Aluminum Green. To Kale's surprise, it was Orange, who had last been seen three months earlier, ten miles to the north, near State Road 50. Leenhouts thought it amazing to have caught him so far from where he was seen and concluded that, unable to find a dusky on the north-of-50 tract, he had flown south in search of companions. Before that, it was assumed that duskies flew no more than a mile. Orange was put in a cloth holding bag and placed in a labeled cardboard box, then transported to Gainesville in an air-conditioned vehicle. Once there, he was released into a twelve by twelve foot cage with several "tutor" Scott's seaside sparrows from the west coast of Florida. They would teach Orange the routine of life in captivity.

Only Aluminum Green now remained on the Beeline Tract. After several unsuccessful attempts to net him, Leenhouts and Sauselein turned their attention to a ranch belonging to Billy Martin, south of State Road 50, where they caught two unbanded birds a week later. Blue and White, as they would be called, joined Orange in Gainesville. The two other males at Gainesville, Red and Yellow, had been captured near State Road 50 the year before.

A short time later the capture team returned to the Beeline in a final attempt to catch the elusive Aluminum Green. They flushed him once but then lost sight of him. This was the last recorded instance of a dusky seaside sparrow in the wild, and in all probability, the last time *anyone* saw one. A disappointed Leenhouts told a reporter, "I played my helmet a lot . . . but he didn't go for it." About every other week, Aluminum Green would cross the Beeline to a tract of land on the other side—the piece Fish and Wildlife had refused to buy a few years earlier. Leenhouts conceded that "the sparrow could have been smashed on the grill of a Greyhound bus while he tried to cross the Beeline." Whatever Aluminum Green's fate, he was not seen again.

For the first time in perhaps ten thousand years, there would be no duskies in the marshes of the St. Johns. But in a wider sense, loss of the dusky signified a decline in the marsh itself. The sparrow had not simply been selectively lifted from its habitat and destroyed. Its disappearance was the most visible symptom of a general malaise. To speak of the dusky was to speak also of the utter transformation of the land where it had evolved. While many justifications would be offered for taking the last duskies in, the real reason was that the accumulation of changes in their habitat meant that there was no safe place left in the world for them outside a cage. Sharp had prophesied as much ten years earlier in the conclusion of his master's thesis when, speaking of the St. Johns, he wrote:

> The towns of Titusville and Cocoa, especially, and even Floridians farther afield, need such a garden; their people are the wealthier for its existence, but will be unfortunate if it is lost. They presently have the opportunity to preserve its delights as their own, or to invade its sanctity, with machines, repetitive houses, and too many people. Far better for us to determine now upon a harmonious distribution of people and landscape, for the ultimate benefit of both, than to have to regret our aesthetic destitution later.

Many people associated with the dusky recovery effort were outlived by the sparrow—or did not live long beyond its extinction. Allan Cruickshank, who had introduced Trost to the dusky and who first proposed the idea for a refuge on Merritt Island, died on October 11, 1974. The trail around a part of the refuge known as Black Point is named in his memory. A year after the capture of the last dusky, Jim Baker's technician Beau Sauselein and a colleague of Beau's, Scott Maness, were killed as they plowed a fire line with a bulldozer around a 100-acre wildfire on Merritt Island in June of 1981. A sudden wind shift whipped the line of fire toward them. They attempted to flee on the dozer, when it got lodged on a stump. They tried frantically to free the machine, then jumped off and ran, taking refuge from the fire in a shallow depression covered in broomgrass. Maness had forgotten his aluminum-blanket fire shelter on the dozer, so they both crawled into Sauselein's, expecting the fire to sweep quickly over the pup tent structure. Burning at several thousand degrees, the fire incinerated the blanket instantaneously. A few minutes later when refuge personnel arrived at the spot, they found Beau and Scott burned beyond recognition. They were rushed to the hospital, where Scott died that evening, Beau the following day. Sauselein's ashes and a wreath of flowers were scattered above the Indian River from a single engine plane. Maness' ashes were tossed in the ocean surf at the edge of the refuge. The new refuge headquarters and visitors' information center is named in their honor.

Not long ago, while going through some old files that Salmela had left at the office of Mosquito Control in Titusville, I opened an envelope and found in it the charred remains of the corner of an aluminum-lined blanket. It was accompanied by Salmela's note: "Remains of Beau Sauselein's emergency blanket." Salmela had picked it up while walking over the charred ground.

On March 11, 1989, ten days after his forty-ninth birthday, Jim Baker, his wife Gail, and some friends rode a ski train into a quiet valley outside of Anchorage, Alaska for a day of cross-country skiing. They disembarked and were gliding on waxed skis beneath the soft winter light, when Baker turned to his wife and gasped, "I think I'm having a heart attack." Moments later he was dead. As he had once requested to his wife, Jim Baker was cremated. She carried his ashes back to his native Mississippi. As an old friend paddled her in a canoe across the still waters of Bluff Lake where Jim and Gail had met, she scattered her husband's ashes among the cypress trees, then dipped her hands to wash them of dust. The remainder of Baker's ashes were buried in an old cemetery in his hometown of Columbus, Mississippi, among the Civil War dead.

The deaths reminded me that the history of the dusky is more than mere chronology. The sparrow's history represents a constellation of individuals' mistakes and fortunes, of their sorrow, their pain. It was Jim Baker slumped in the Alaskan snow; and Beau Sauselein and Scott Maness huddled helplessly together against a wildfire. It was the last song of Aluminum Green, piercing the silence in an ancient land of water and grass.

18

To Recreate a Sparrow

Immediately after their capture, the duskies became wards of the state, maintained by the Florida Game and Fresh Water Fish Commission at its research laboratories near Gainesville, where Fish and Wildlife provided funds for their keeping.

For the next two years they would live as foster children, shunted from home to home, with no long-range plans for their well-being or the future of their kind. Living in a gray world of overlapping jurisdictions, they belonged to no one. They were growing older, and their future possibilities were limited. Fish and Wildlife hoped a female might yet be found in the wild to mother a new generation of birds. Short of this remote possibility, the duskies could be kept captive until they died; they could be released and reclaimed by nature; or the males could be crossbred with females of a closely related kind of seaside sparrow, such as the Scott's seaside sparrow from the Florida Gulf Coast, to yield dusky-like offspring—an experiment that Fish and Wildlife refused to authorize.

In theory, an almost pure dusky could eventually be created through "backcrossing." A pure male dusky mated with a pure Scott's female would produce offspring that were, on average, half dusky and half Scott's. If you mated one of these "50 percenter" females with another pure dusky male, you would end up with a bird three-quarters dusky, and one-quarter Scott's. Take this 75 percenter and backcross it with yet another of the male pure duskies, and you'd end up with a bird 87.5 percent dusky. And so forth and so on, until after five generations a bird almost 97 percent dusky would be produced. In effect, the genetics of backcrossing is analogous to mixing two colors of paint, adding more and more of one color until the other is almost totally diluted out. Over several generations, the Scott's could be mostly diluted out of the offspring, and an almost pure dusky would be created. But little was known about keeping any kind of seaside sparrow in captivity, let alone about breeding and hybridizing them.

In the late 1970s, before the final duskies were captured, the Santa Fe Community College Teaching Zoo in Gainesville had experimented with Scott's sparrows in aviaries. They would serve as a model for the dusky. After a short time in captivity, the birds successfully bred, marking the first known breeding of any type of seaside sparrow in captivity.

The Florida Game and Fresh Water Fish Commission, meanwhile, had in its possession several Scott's as well as three duskies that had been captured in 1979. The scenario there was ripe for the ultimate experiment—crossbreeding Scott's with duskies. As luck would have it, the male duskies and female Scott's lived in neighboring cages. A female Scott's "escaped" into a cage holding the pure dusky known as "Red." They mated, and by May 14, 1980, three eggs had been laid in a nest built in a clump of broomgrass within the aviary. Three healthy half-dusky offspring hatched. All three fledged. Fish and Game biologist Will Post called the incident a "happy accident." Actually, many people suspected that this was no accident; it had only been made to appear so in the hope of avoiding Fish and Wildlife's wrath. Authorized or not, the crossbreeding answered an important question: the dusky and the Scott's could be hybridized. A short time later, one of the hybrid females mated with a Scott's male and laid fertile eggs—proving that the dusky–Scott's hybrid was fertile. A near calamity followed. In 1979 a rat snake entered the cage and ate one of the Scott's. (Another snake had broken in previously but, fortunately, none of the duskies was eaten.)

Even as scientific questions were put to bed, troubling political ones were just awakening. Fish and Wildlife officials were not eager to further complicate the issue of endangered species with a multifarious debate about man-made hybrids. No one even knew if the dusky–Scott's would be protected under the Endangered Species Act. Even if they were, such a project could only compromise the service's strained budget. Fish and Wildlife would have preferred to avoid the question of the hybrid duskies all together, but faced with a growing prohybrid coalition, chose the next most expedient course: it pretended to argue the issue on scientific merit, while selectively marshalling the "facts" to support its antihybrid agenda. Once again, the aims of politics were set on a collision course with the goals of science.

The scientific community was confident at the prospect of "recreating" the dusky by backcrossing. Thomas E. Lovejoy, a vice president for World Wildlife Fund, stated the case in a letter to Ron Lambertson, associate director of Federal Assistance for Fish and Wildlife: "I feel the backcrossing effort is very important as a demonstration of what can be done when other efforts have failed for whatever reason and only a small single-sex population remains. . . . I fail to see how Fish and Wildlife can spend so much on ducks and then fret about the costs [associated with backcrossing]. We haven't even expected money for the backcrossing; all we want is an okay."

The International Council for Bird Preservation also urged Fish and Wildlife to approve backcrossing, charging that "the remaining duskies have been relegated to living out their time celibate and in captivity, a slightly less expensive alternative [than breeding them.]" After several unsuccessful attempts to get Fish and Wildlife to change its stand, Jon M. Jensen, executive director of Wildlife Preservation Trust International, wrote to Will Post: "It is unfortunate that we could not come to terms with Fish and Wildlife, but come to terms with them we must."

On June 20, 1980, representatives from a number of organizations, including Fish and Wildlife, met on Merritt Island and unanimously concluded that crossbreeding should be initiated by the Florida Game and Fresh Water Fish Commission. Voting in favor of the proposal were Lovett Williams, his colleague Will Post, as well as Harold O'Connor, who by now had risen to the post of deputy associate director for Federal Assistance, the branch of Fish and Wildlife with jurisdiction over the Endangered Species Program. O'Connor had managed the Merritt Island Refuge from 1969 to 1972. Herb Kale was exultant about the decision.

But when the executive director of the commission, Colonel Robert M. Brantly, heard about the plan, he immediately wrote to Regional Director Black in Atlanta, explaining, "We have certain philosophical reservations regarding such a program. Producing hybrids is outside the objective of our Endangered Wildlife Project and in my opinion ineffective as a means of preserving a taxon." Black wrote back to Brantly disavowing the entire notion of crossbreeding: "The recommendations that came out of that meeting, in my opinion, were not the Fish and Wildlife's recommendations but recommendations to Fish and Wildlife and State from the group of experts that attended the meeting . . . Fish and Wildlife's position will be . . . no crossbreeding or hybridization of the dusky seaside sparrow." Black seemed to have forgotten that O'Connor attended the meeting as a high-level Fish and Wildlife representative. Indeed, a second Fish and Wildlife employee at the meeting, Harold Benson, also advocated crossbreeding.

Black then called the director of Fish and Wildlife in Washington, Lynn Greenwalt, and explained that the notion of crossbreeding was ludicrous. Black's first concern was that it might be illegal to use money earmarked for one endangered species to, in effect, "create a new one." As far as Black was concerned, the dusky seaside sparrow was already extinct, for without females, the species had no future; the time had come to ". . . forget about the sparrow and get on with our work." He believed the world to be

> . . . full of people who believe you should do *anything* for an endangered species. Animals have always gone extinct, but when man becomes part of the equation, extinction takes place much more rapidly. When it comes to the rescue operation of endangered species, triage must be part of the process, although few people in a position of authority in Fish and Wildlife have the political courage to admit it. The fact is, money is earmarked on the basis of what species present the greatest chance of success. With the dusky we were throwing good money after bad.

O'Connor, meanwhile, apparently underwent a conversion on his return to Washington and soon came out against crossbreeding. He explained his change of mind to a *Los Angeles Times* reporter: "For me it was a particularly difficult decision. Like everyone in attendance [at the meeting], I was extremely excited about the possibility of crossbreeding. . . . Emotions tell you one thing. Economic necessity, logic, and hard decision are something else."

Bill Leenhouts also attended the June meeting and enthusiastically supported the notion of crossbreeding. He interpreted the sudden change of stance toward the project as symptomatic of the bureaucracy itself: "After that meeting, a lot of service people went back to Washington to recommend crossbreeding. As soon as the idea hit the bureaucracy, people stopped looking at the possibilities in crossbreeding and started dwelling on its potential political liabilities. It is always safer to say no because it's hard to fail when you do nothing. The idea is to maximize your minimum losses."

In a broader sense, according to Leenhouts:

> Fish and Wildlife's stand against crossbreeding was in reality a politically acceptable way of instituting triage. The dusky was never going to get any funding because it wasn't bigger than a bread box and offered no compelling reason, beyond its own value, for saving it. The dusky deserved to be saved and there is really no compelling reason it should not have been. But we cannot save all endangered animals and the dusky was one of them. Fish and Wildlife wasn't going to come out and use the word triage, but that's what it was.

Black, now retired, recently told me from his summer home in Idaho, "I don't regret my decision not to crossbreed. I'd say that one of the first criteria in choosing an animal to save is the possibility of success. You shouldn't be throwing good money after bad. It is effectively a policy of triage. A lot of people would be horrified by this. It would not surprise me if no one in a position of responsibility within Fish and Wildlife would say that. It would take a lot of guts to avow triage publicly."

In other words, faced with limited resources and a burgeoning number of endangered animals, Fish and Wildlife would have to choose which species to try to salvage and which to allow to die. For every dollar spent on the dusky, an endangered species somewhere else would languish with a dollar less. Whatever Fish and Wildlife's failure in the application of sound scientific principles, this was also a failure of political nerve—to publicly admit to the policy that it was actively carrying out. With colossal mistakes having been made at almost every step of the way in the aborted effort to save the dusky, the sparrow now was to be given up for lost.

Whatever Fish and Wildlife's misgivings about publicly stating why it rejected hybridization, Kale railed against the stand: "I am disgusted—neither the regional nor federal director wants to allow crossbreeding of the remaining surviving male duskies (five in captivity in Gainesville, one still loose in the wild); instead, they will allow them to die in captivity."

The Florida Audubon Society sent a resolution its members had passed to Director Greenwalt, warning that "the gene pool of the unique population of seaside sparrows will be lost forever with the death of these surviving males," and urged Fish and Wildlife to include a program of crossbreeding and backcrossing in an effort to reinstate a viable dusky seaside sparrow population.

Greenwalt and Black remained adamant, and in response to the resolution, O'Connor informed the president of the Florida Audubon Society, "As you know, last year the Florida Game and Fresh Water Fish Commission carried out a captive propagation project using dusky and Scott's seaside sparrows, two closely related subspecies. Fish and Wildlife, however, takes the position that . . . hybrid progeny would not be legally protected under the Endangered Species Act of 1973, as amended. For these reasons, we have no plans to become involved in a crossbreeding project."

In fact, there was already a highly successful precedent for such hybridization that was wholeheartedly supported by Fish and Wildlife. The recovery of the peregrine falcon was based on the crossbreeding of the American peregrine with several subspecies, including one from Europe—common knowledge among service employees. Leenhouts had scrawled on the bottom of a Fish and Wildlife memo that reiterated the agency's position against crossbreeding, "Too bad everyone is throwing in the towel. We hybridized peregrines and no one squawked."

In 1981 Fish and Wildlife hardened its position and informed Kale that the five surviving sparrows—Yellow, Orange, Red, White, and Blue—would be taken from the state control all together and moved to the teaching zoo at Santa Fe Community College in Gainesville. There a "maintenance" program was established—in effect an old age home for the birds. Many believed it would be the sparrows' final resting place. Jim Ellis, curator of Santa Fe Community College Teaching Zoo, saw little in the way of a future for the birds. He was quoted as saying, "We hope we can learn something from them that will help us save another species in the future." According to *Gainesville Sun* reporter Joanne Fanizza, when Tony Blalock, director of technical education at Santa Fe Community College, said the college would receive more than $40,000 for the first year to support the birds, board of trustee member J. M. Brownlee incited laughter when he quipped, "Eight thousand dollars a year room and board for a sparrow! You should get a nice profit on it."

Will Post and Lovett Williams were infuriated by the decision to move the birds—especially by the agreement's implication: Fish and Wildlife, taking the politically expedient course, had resigned itself to allowing the birds to die in captivity.

Said Post:

> The people at the regional level of Fish and Wildlife are chicken shits—small-minded people fighting for their own local survival by keeping their supervisors happy. Fish and Wildlife cut off funds to the Game and Fish Commission because they didn't like the idea of crossbreeding, which they said couldn't be done. When we proved that it was feasible, they said if those idiots can do it, anyone can do it. They wanted their fingers in the pie. If anything was going to be accomplished, they wanted full credit. In my opinion, they intentionally destroyed our breeding program because their people couldn't afford politically to see it succeed without them. They first took away our funding, then they took away the birds.

In fact, Fish and Wildlife was not only incensed at the unauthorized crossbreeding of the sparrows but fed up with getting routinely lambasted by Kale and other determined advocates of crossbreeding. Fish and Wildlife explained that it would be holding the male duskies for two more years while an intensive search for females was conducted. If a female dusky was found, it would be captured for a propagation effort. If a female wasn't found, Fish and Wildlife might reevaluate its stand against backcrossing—notwithstanding the fact that thorough searches for females had already been made. Baker had searched for female duskies throughout the late 1970s. He was still looking for them, without success, when Trost and Sharp arrived for the 1979 conference. One Fish and Wildlife employee told a *New York Times* reporter that keeping the remaining five birds in captivity was actually "a public relations deal" to protect Fish and Wildlife from criticism had the birds been returned to the refuge to die in their natural habitat.

Jim Ellis felt that Fish and Wildlife was making the only rational choice. "Emotions were incredibly intense," he later explained to me. "Neither side would budge. Somebody had to take control of the situation, and that's what Fish and Wildlife did. Their first priority was to get out from under the crossbreeding controversy, clear the air and then to evaluate the situation. It was a dangerous time."

Others failed to see the logic in holding five males captive for two years while biologists searched for females—especially when the chance of finding them was nil. Warren King urged that if crossbreeding wasn't going to be allowed, then the birds should be released back into the wild along with some Scott's sparrows rather than waste their remaining years in captivity. Kale, however, suspected that such a reasonable proposal would go over with Fish and Wildlife like "a lead balloon."

While the duskies went to Santa Fe, the three 50 percenters begotten from the "accidental" mating at the Game and Fish Commission were sent, along with the Scott's, to hastily constructed aviaries at the behavior laboratories of the Florida State Museum, where John W. Hardy, curator in Ornithology and Bioaccoustics, agreed to take them in. The pure duskies, meanwhile, were living out their days with Fish and Wildlife support across town.

In March of 1981, Hardy sent to the Endangered Species Office of Fish and Wildlife in Washington a proposal for crossbreeding in which "no funds are requested . . . it is our intention to use approval of the Fish and Wildlife to generate funds from private sources."

Inexplicably, Fish and Wildlife replied with a letter denying funds for such a project. The author of the rejection, F. Eugene Hester, acting deputy director of Fish and Wildlife in Washington, went on to cite several specific arguments against crossbreeding. Then he explained that as an alternative to crossbreeding, sperm from the duskies would be frozen and stored at Fish and Wildlife's Patuxent Wildlife Research Center. Hardy was beside himself. He had not even asked for funding—only that permission be given to use the male duskies. In his vitriolic style, Hardy fired back: ". . . I judge each point [you made] to be either demonstrably unsupportable, theoretically weak, or beside the point."

First, to Hester's argument that "There is no assurance that hybridization will produce fertile dusky-like seaside sparrows," Hardy reminded him of the three dusky hybrids already produced at the University of Florida and that the male is

> . . . so close to the dusky phenotype that it would pass for a dusky in the field without question. . . . [As for the hybrids not accepting the habitat or of them being infertile] Your pessimistic position on these two points is understandable, but the results are in and you are wrong. The . . . hybrids readily accepted our artificial aviary salt marshes here in Gainesville—indicating that stability of habitat broadly resembling native habitat is all that is required.

Time and time again, the service would raise the question of the hybrids' adaptability to the wild. S. Dillon Ripley, president of the International Council for Bird Preservation at the Smithsonian Institution in Washington, called the issue ". . . irrelevant: Sparrows as a species are rather specific in certain kinds of dense, brackish and saltwater grasses, and can hardly be described to be so intolerant of the remaining salt marsh habitats in Florida as to die out once reintroduced for matters of biological preference. They could, of course, die out for objective problems, such as sprays, interference of various kinds, or destruction of the habitat itself."

As for Hester's second point—the viability of offspring—Hardy continued:

> *The birds are fertile.* Two of the sibling crosses were placed together in one aviary and have successfully nested, producing two fledglings. The third was placed in another aviary with a male Scott's seaside sparrow and they have also produced two fledglings. One bird accidentally drowned but the other three are doing quite well.

Hardy then went on to attack Hester's other arguments against crossbreeding:

> You speak . . . as if you believe there is a pure genotype that we call the dusky seaside sparrow that is utterly distinct from other genotypes of other races of the seaside sparrow. By the very definition of subspecies or race this is utterly fallacious, and I am surprised that there are not dozens of trained zoologists on your staff who have not objected to your misunderstanding. . . . Indeed, it is quite possible, perhaps even likely, that the dusky seaside sparrow differs from other seaside sparrows only in the gene for intensity of pigmentation.
>
> Let me assure you that persistence of officials of the Office of Endangered Species in supporting this "purity of the races" concept has much potential for doing irreparable damage to the endangered species program as it might succeed through captive propagation. The position is far removed from reasonable premises of science.
>
> All the information that exists is 100% indicative that backcrossing of hybrids to duskies is feasible. . . . As for the belief that backcrossing of successive generations of hybrids to dusky males will produce generations each on average closer to pure dusky genotype . . . well, that is just standard,

elementary, textbook probability math, no more no less. Check it out. . . . Yet to deny the captive backcross propagation, now, with living duskies, with only cryogenesis or the discovery of a female dusky to fall back on seems to me to be simply irresponsible.

Meanwhile, with no pure duskies to work with, Hardy desperately forged ahead with hybridizing the three 50 percenters (only full duskies were subject to Fish and Wildlife's control) and the full Scott's. In the spring of 1981, a female 50 percenter mated with a Scott's male. The remaining brother and sister 50 percenters from the successful clutch at Fish and Game in 1979 were also paired. Both pairs produced clutches in April, May, and June, laying at least eighteen eggs. Twelve of the eggs hatched. Within a month after hatching, four of the fledglings had either mysteriously disappeared or died. Norwegian rats and yellow rat snakes had managed to tunnel under and enter the hastily built aviaries, possibly using mole burrows. Another fledgling choked to death. But the greatest catastrophe of all occurred on June 23, 1981, when Norwegian rats again got into the enclosure, destroyed both pairs' nests, ate the eggs, and killed three of the four breeders. One of the females was found torn to pieces in her nest.

Another of the fledglings flew into the wide end of a space between one wooden beam and the mesh, worked itself toward the narrow end until it was so tightly stuck it could not move. It was found flattened and dead there. The corpse was removed, and while it was being examined another hybrid flew into the same space and nearly suffered the same fate. It was rescued and the space sealed. By the end of the 1981 breeding season, not a single offspring of the two pairings had survived. Hardy blamed the invasion of predators into the cages on "pressures of time and lack of funds."

After these mishaps, one of the researchers concluded, "Our advice to the seaside sparrow aviculturist is to assume constantly that the worst and most improbable disasters are waiting to happen, and to plan accordingly. The seasides should be housed the way a jail warden would house an ingenious and deranged criminal determined to commit suicide."

Fish and Wildlife, meanwhile, continued to argue that the 1973 Endangered Species Act did not cover hybrids, a view that Florida State University professor Frances C. James called "inconsistent with modern biology. . . . The introgression of genes among populations is a biological process that goes on all the time in nature."

Fish and Wildlife had actually confronted the question of hybrids and the Endangered Species Act in 1977 in connection with the endangered red wolf, believed to be a hybrid. In April that year the chief of the Division of Law Enforcement of Fish and Wildlife in Washington wrote to the solicitor at the regional office, asking whether "a hybrid of an endangered or threatened species is covered by the Endangered Species Act of 1973." The response by Assistant Solicitor Ronald Lambertson was unequivocal:

> For the purposes of the act, a "hybrid of an endangered or threatened species" may be defined as the offspring of two animals or two plants where each parent is from a different species and where at least one parent is from an endangered or threatened species. . . . The language of the statute, its legislative history, and one of the law's purposes indicate that hybrids of endangered or threatened species are covered by the act. Because it defines "fish or wildlife" to include any offspring without limitation, the Act's plain meaning dictates coverage of hybrids of listed animal species. The legislative history buttresses this conclusion. . . . It is clear, therefore, that the Act's policy of reducing commerce in listed species will be greatly frustrated if hybrids of such species are not covered by the act.

In short, any offspring, even if only *one* of the parents was an endangered species, comes under protection of the act. The ruling was in keeping with the hybridization of the peregrine falcon. But the dusky was rationalized to be different. When O'Connor saw the ruling, he wrote back to the solicitor to dispute the legal finding:

> . . . the opinion places us in a biologically unsound position. Further, we find it difficult to believe that the original intent of the Congress was other than to have the offspring of endangered species classed as endangered only when both parents are endangered. We do not believe their intent was to have offspring classed as endangered when only one parent was endangered and the other was an unlisted species. . . . Wise management would dictate that we should proceed to eliminate or at least separate the hybrids from the pure strain to prevent interbreeding. . . . If we are prevented from following this course of action because of the classification of the hybrids, we would again find a situation where the species was suffering because of a legal interpretation of the act's meaning . . . since the act was clearly passed to benefit endangered species, it is our feeling that this section must have meant the offspring of two listed species and not meant to protect a hybrid where that protection would in fact cause jeopardy to the continued existence of the species. . . . It would be extremely helpful if we could have this opinion reconsidered as soon as possible.

On August 2, 1977, Acting Assistant Solicitor Donald J. Barry, who had replaced Lambertson, wrote back granting O'Connor's request. Explaining that he had "received additional biological information from your office," Barry wrote that, in fact, coverage of hybrids in the act would

> . . . hinder the conservation of endangered or threatened species and possibly jeopardize their continued existence. . . . While the language concerning the definition of "fish and

wildlife" . . . may on its face indicate coverage of hybrids, the harmful effects of such coverage discussed earlier make that language at least latently ambiguous.

In a matter of days, interpretation of the law had undergone a radical reversal. Initially, conservation would be greatly frustrated "if hybrids . . . are not covered by the act." A week later, extending protection to hybrids would "hinder the conservation of endangered or threatened species." Fish and Wildlife had cast out sound reasoning in order to dictate its own interpretation of the law. A frustrated Kale wrote to Defenders of Wildlife: "The decision not to crossbreed is based on economics and selective solicitors' opinions, not on biological or ethical grounds. . . . All that is left to do now is prepare an obituary for the population."

Harold O'Connor, meanwhile, continued his ascent within the hierarchy, eventually becoming director of Patuxent Wildlife Research Center, one of the highest positions within Fish and Wildlife overseeing endangered species.

19

Bureaucracy

In September 1981, Ms. H. L. Keenan, a concerned citizen from West Palm Beach, wrote to Fish and Wildlife's Jacksonville office to ask why the hybridization proposal had been rejected. Fielding the letter was Assistant Area Manager for Endangered Species, David W. Peterson, who also oversaw the duskies at Santa Fe Community College. Peterson wrote back to Ms. Keenan: "I did have the opportunity to review and comment on [the] proposal, and, to be honest, recommended against it." He went on to explain in two and a half pages why he opposed hybridization. According to his argument—to use the mixed paint analogy—identical gray paints mixed together would yield not the same color gray, but one inexplicably lighter. He wrote:

> If one 94% dusky bred with another 94% dusky the offspring—theoretically—would only be 88% dusky. The next generation 78% dusky, and so on down the line until you ended up with a 50-50 mix of dusky and Scott's.

As it so happened, Keenan sent John Hardy at the Florida State Museum both a copy of her original letter as well as Peterson's reply. Hardy went berserk when he read it and wrote a blistering riposte to Peterson, stating that his explanation of what happens to 94 percent duskies if they inbreed is "embarrassingly incorrect." Indeed, Peterson had erroneously concluded that backcrossing of offspring would diminish the dusky genes at each generation. Continued Hardy:

> I find it sickening that you were, armed with such misinformation, allowed an opinion of whether we would have been allowed to do the captive breeding. . . . The continuing failure of high-ranking officials in the top administrative and god help us decision-making offices of the U.S. Fish and Wildlife Service to demonstrate much more than a layman's grasp of basic biological principles is a source of utter amazement and despair to me. To compound that problem by disseminating misinformation based on a woeful misgrasp of the facts to concerned citizens without first "checking the facts" with a knowledgeable biologist (of which you employ many at the hands-on level) is simply irresponsibility defined.

At the bottom of the page Hardy scribbled in longhand, "Copies to *everybody*."

Fish and Wildlife stuck to its promise to continue searching for female duskies. To no one's surprise, extensive surveys in the St. Johns in the spring and summer of 1981 turned up none. After this, Hardy was confident that Fish and Wildlife would cry uncle. In early September he wrote again to the director, explaining that if a breeding program were to be undertaken the following spring, permission would have to be granted by November 1.

In early October—Hardy had still not heard from Fish and Wildlife—the North Carolina Biological Survey and Fish and Wildlife sponsored a symposium on the seaside sparrow, in Raleigh, North Carolina. At the conference Kale met Fish and Wildlife Acting Director Eugene Hester (who had signed the letter to Hardy rejecting his crossbreeding proposal), and was confident that he would reply fairly—if not favorably—to Hardy's request. Kale was impressed with Hester, and in a letter to him shortly after the symposium, described him as an "intelligent, friendly, and straightforward human being. I was greatly relieved to learn that not everyone nowadays is a horror story out of Washington." Hester had received his Ph.D. in zoology from Auburn University in 1959, the same year Hardy had received his from the University of Kansas. At the meeting, Kale urged Hester to act on Hardy's new proposal by the deadline of November 1, and then, in a follow-up letter, stated, "If you are going to once again deny this request I hope your explanation will be scientifically and intellectually open and honest. I'm confident that if you are personally involved with this decision that it will be just that, regardless of the outcome."

Kale hoped to insure that Hester was personally involved in the decision because it had become embarrassingly clear that Hester hadn't actually written the responses to Hardy's requests in the first place, even though the correspondence bore his signature. The letters apparently had been ghost-written by his staff. Or, if Hester did write them, he didn't remember much of their contents. When asked during the symposium why he opposed the crossbreeding, Hester couldn't come up with a single one of the five points he had made in an earlier letter to Hardy. This only furthered Hardy's suspicion that the federal endangered species program was managed not by experts, but by faceless bureaucrats who only now and again stepped forward to show themselves.

Kale knew that, among other things, for Fish and Wildlife to be "scientifically and intellectually open and honest" would require Hester to admit that the arguments against crossbreeding were essentially political, not scientific or legal.

Kale hoped that Hester could get beyond Fish and Wildlife's entrenched black-and-white mentality and realize that a "subspecies" is a working definition, not some exact category defined by nature. Rather, subspecies are an invention taxonomists use to help them organize life's overwhelming diversity. If Fish and Wildlife could loosen up its definition of subspecies, then the service would see that hybridization was not Frankensteinian; it was not unlike something nature herself often tried, albeit over many generations.

S. Dillon Ripley wrote to James G. Watt, then secretary of the interior under President Ronald Reagan, that Fish and Wildlife's view of the dusky as a subspecies was "based on legalisms with regard to the regulations themselves enacted by the hand of human beings, rather than [by] the hand of God. The populations of subspecies in such closely related forms as the seaside sparrow can never be manipulated by man, as if indeed they were inviolate, and acts of a separate creation. Subspecies are at best a subjective concept of human beings. . . . Thus a considerable amount of the man-made legislation creating endangered subspecies can only be assumed to be a transitory phenomenon, as transitory perhaps as a house of cards."

Ripley sounded a similar note in a letter to John Spinks, chief of the Office of Endangered Species of Fish and Wildlife in Washington, and said, "With regard to the dusky seaside sparrow, it seems obvious to me that the only solution is to breed the surviving males to captured females of a subspecies from Florida of this species." He went on record on behalf of the International Council of Bird Preservation strongly supporting the concepts already supported by Wildlife Preservation Trust International, World Wildlife Fund, and Safari International. Ripley warned that, "It may well be that the time lag in discussion, arbitration and indecision of the authorities concerned may succeed in wiping out the remaining population. If so the question will resolve itself in a negative manner, which will eliminate the problem. However, I cannot believe that the Office of Endangered Species is primarily concerned in rapid extinction of endangered subspecies . . . as I understand it, [breeding] is already too late for the year 1981. Let us, of course, assume only that the surviving males will still be alive at that time [next year]."

Some within the scientific community had begun to liken Fish and Wildlife's opposition to a bird of mixed blood as the biological equivalent of racism. Kale wrote to a friend at the National Zoological Park in Washington, D.C., explaining that Frances C. James of the Department of Biological Science at Florida State University had sent a letter to *BioScience* that will "lambast the Fish and Wildlife for racism and ignorance of population genetics. I hope it is published soon." It was. James wrote, "This is a case of the government's becoming trapped in a semantic web of its own creation. The federal definition of a *species* is a nightmare of prose and conflicts with the species concept as used by biologists. . . . The legal position that the dusky seaside sparrow . . . is a 'pure race,' and that a captive breeding program that uses females from another subspecies is ineligible for support under the Endangered Species Act, is not consistent with modern biology. Such reasoning, applied to a human population, would be called racism or miscegenation."

Hardy, meanwhile, impatiently waited for Hester to reply before the November 1 deadline. The reply never came. Three days after his proposed deadline, a miffed Hardy wrote to the director of Fish and Wildlife, still complaining about the June 1980 meeting in which the service initially urged crossbreeding:

> Let me say that from your office on down through the ranks, I believe a number of officials acted about this whole matter in a casual and irresponsible manner. That began with oral statements to Peter Mott of Florida Audubon and Dr. Frances James of Florida State University that a captive breeding program *would be* approved, which prompted a group of scientists and other officials to engage in weeks of planning and negotiation, when in fact the original oral statements had been made lightly and with no authority.

In this letter, Hardy couldn't resist bringing up the incident that had occurred at the seaside sparrow symposium held in Raleigh:

> That Mr. Hester was merely a signer of the letter and was not involved in whatever thought went into the five points became laughably (or lamentably) clear when at the Raleigh, NC symposium on the seaside sparrow he could not, when queried, even remember what the five denial points were! How sad. . . . I think that from the director on down you ought to be thoroughly ashamed of yourself. It is my intention in the coming months to see that as many people as possible know of your apparent inadequacies; I hope that will include your superiors.

With the crucial decision made against crossbreeding, the birds would remain in limbo for two years at Santa Fe. Kenneth Black retired in 1982, and still no female sparrows had been found. With two critical years in which no young were produced, the sparrow was two years closer to extinction. At that point, Fish and Wildlife wrote to Kale suggesting that "Florida Audubon look into the probability of fostering a breeding project for the 1983 breeding season." Fish and Wildlife made it clear that any offspring would not be protected by the Endangered Species Act, nor would the service "provide any funding to support this crossbreeding project nor allow the release of offspring on any national wildlife refuge." If Audubon didn't come up with a proposal by the end of fiscal year 1983, the last dusky seaside sparrows would be released back to the wild. Fish and Wildlife had made its case against hybridization. Now someone else could worry about what to do with the sparrows.

20

Magic Kingdom

Charlie Cook, thirty-four, rose early on September 27, 1983. He had spent the night in Gainesville with two friends, preparing himself for one of the most important days of his life. That morning he would drive the last four living dusky seaside sparrows from their temporary home in Gainesville to permanent quarters in aviaries at Walt Disney World near Orlando. Cook felt like the chosen one. As he headed out the door, his friends bid him good luck. Then one of them surprised him with four chiffon green sacks that she had sewn from pillow cases and hand-embroidered in yellow thread with the words Sparrow 1, Sparrow 2, Sparrow 3, and Sparrow 4. The top of each was closed with a cinch. Cook took the sacks gratefully, climbed into a white Chevrolet sedan borrowed from the Disney World motorpool and headed outside of town to the Santa Fe Teaching Zoo, where the last duskies had resided since their capture on the St. Johns two years earlier.

Cook was born in Lakeland, Florida, about a half hour from Disney World, and he had never ventured more than a couple of days' drive from his hometown. In the early 1970s he attended Lee College in Cleveland, Tennessee, majored in theology, and left after completing his junior year. He next worked for a year in a Lakeland halfway house as a counselor of runaway youths, before taking a job as an animal keeper at Disney World's Blackbeard's Island in Bay Lake, near Cinderella's Castle. The attraction would later become Discovery Island. Because the water of Bay Lake stores heat, the acre-and-a-half island is noticeably warmer than the surrounding areas on chilly days and proved to be an ideal loca tion for keeping many tropical plants and animals. Discovery Island was soon home to the largest captive flock of the rare scarlet ibis in the world and received accreditation by the American Association of Zoological Parks and Aquariums in 1981. Discovery Island would become the sparrows' final home.

Cook had come to Discovery Island when he was 21, unsure of where his life was leading. He sometimes sat on an old fallen live oak on the island, anxiously weeping over what his future would hold. By 1975 he had become curator of Discovery Island. Cook became involved in various projects at Disney World. Among other activities, he oversaw the installation of a $250,000 parrot cage, designed in Italy and hand-built of English birch, that now graces the lobby of the Grand Floridian Resort Hotel at Disney World. Eight feet high and four feet square, with inner bars of fine piano wire concealed by an outer cage of polished brass rods, the ornate Italianate style cage became home to several brilliantly pink hybrid Rosy Borke parakeets.

Cook seemed to embrace a system of beliefs that made him a natural to work for Walt Disney World. Cook believed in an orderly universe. The ultimate optimist, he believed good fortune to be a blessing, hardship a blessing in disguise. He was the ultimate Noah; he was the incomparable Job. He told me, "One day I was sitting on a fallen tree crying. Next thing I know, I am steward of the last dusky seaside sparrows on earth."

As Cook headed out the door that morning, if he did not cherish the unexpected role, he nevertheless embraced it. Through no planning of his own, he had become master, godfather, and pope to the last remaining individuals of a race of bird. Cook said, "I knew my life would change because they were so precious. They were truly the best thing for a person like me, who loved to see nature, could ever hope to hold in his hand. They were the best because I knew that they were like untold stories—they were the real thing, as real as anything could be. They were awesome."

When he arrived at the Santa Fe Teaching Zoo at eight o'clock, the keeper netted the birds and placed them each in a sack, and then carefully placed each on the back seat of the sedan. Ellis was also present, and a friend captured the moment on video tape. One old bird, Blue, was having such difficulty breathing that no one was quite sure he could survive the trip. He did. Cook named Blue "Abraham" because "he looked a little tired and ragged and was expected, like the biblical figure, to father a new generation, despite his age." He didn't.

Orange, on the other hand, was curious, quick to fly up from the broomgrass in his cage and to see what was going on. Although young in spirit, he was, according to records, among the oldest of the captives. For all the birds' heightened worth, captivity marked the fatal threshold.

Unfortunately, one of the five captives passed away only weeks before Cook arrived. Feathers fluffed in an effort to keep warm, Red began labored breathing through his opened bill. On Saturday morning, September 11, after falling from his perch to the ground, Red was placed in an oxygen tent and was rushed across town to the veterinary school at the University of Florida. The sparrow was dead on arrival. A necropsy revealed that a large tumor had invaded Red's abdomen and chest cavity. There would be only four sparrows to take to Disney World.

Some time after Red's death, Refuge Manager Vehrs inquired of the Florida Game and Fresh Water Fish Commission about getting a dusky to put on display at Merritt Island National Wildlife Refuge visitor center: "With regard to mounting, we are both interested in obtaining the best product. I understand you are extremely pleased with your taxidermist. We also are very confident in the ability of ours. If we can come to some agreement, I would like to select the best taxidermist for the job." The honor of public display would be Red's, who got stuffed. There he would remain on display for several years—until "attacked" by marauding rats that had gotten behind the glass.

Orange, Yellow, White, and Blue were comfortably ensconced in the backseat of the car, heading toward Orlando. Cook was nervous; to him the birds represented a "rip in the fabric of the universe." They lay silently in the sacks, chirping only if nudged. That was the hard part. Unless he nudged them they wouldn't move. The object was not to bother them or stress them at all. After fifteen or twenty minutes nothing moved; he wondered if they were alive. A tank of oxygen and an aquarium that could be fitted with a lid and turned into an oxygen "tent" was at the ready in the back seat. The death of one of the sparrows was only one of his concerns. It could not be allowed to decay if it died. About midway down the turnpike, Cook pulled over at a predetermined spot, saw that the birds were okay, and continued toward Orlando.

Then it was off the turnpike at Ocala, through the town

of Winter Gardens and through the back gate of Disney World. He drove to the boat dock where the blue-pennant boat leaves for Discovery Island, loaded the birds aboard, and motored to the island. With little publicity or fanfare, the birds were released into their aviaries. Blue had made it. At last the duskies, who had seen two homes since their removal from the wild, had found a permanent resting place. Cook breathed a deep sigh of relief.

Cook placed the duskies in the aviary that had been painstakingly built the preceding year; a half dozen of a more common type of seaside sparrow had been used to test for "leaks" and other sorts of structural problems. Workers had built six screen-covered cages, each ten by ten feet, within a larger wire-mesh-covered structure—cages within a cage. One needed to pass through two doors to enter the larger facility, and yet through another door to actually get inside the sparrows' cage. The bottom of each cage was covered with a foot of sand planted with broomgrass. The plants were sprinkled with salt, as they would have been back on Merritt Island and in the St. Johns. An overhead sprinkler system, turned on daily, simulated the summer showers of the natural marsh. Small oval cement pools were sunk into the ground near the broomgrass, and fresh water trickled through them, as a little rivulet forms after a shower. Flashing was buried in the ground around the facility to keep burrowing predators, such as rats, from getting inside. A tall sweet gum tree stood outside at the northern end. Over the palmettos and beyond the lake rose the three turrets of Cinderella's Castle. Although scarcely a hundred feet from the visitors' path winding through the island, the cages were hidden behind the walls of palmetto and grass.

The head keeper, Lisa Danforth, came to the cages at seven each morning to feed the captives a mixture of canary seed soaked in water and wheat germ oil. This was set in a dish on the tiny island in the water trough to keep it away from ants. Every afternoon each bird was fed ten crickets and five mealworms. Inside the aviary Danforth wore special boots and a special outer garment used only within the cages. Each spring afternoon, an attendant walked to the cages with Cook's cassette and played a sparrow song a minute long to stimulate the male's singing. The birds were safe from a dangerous world. They could grow old and die in peace if not in the dignity their native habitat might have offered. Cook was relieved, but more than once he visited the captives and asked, "Where to now, Lord?"

21

Final Rest

D oes it seem strange that Disney World should rescue a
sparrow whose marshland home had been destroyed by
humans? In *Bambi*, when the fawn asks his mother why all
the deer fled the meadow where they had come to graze, she
replies that "man" is in the forest. And as evil in the film
was ultimately overcome by good, Cook believed the dusky
seaside sparrow would ultimately prevail in real life. So it
was in 1983, after Kale had enlisted Cook and Walt Disney
World to support efforts to hybridize the sparrows, that the
last duskies had come to Discovery Island.

Audubon president Peter R. Mott had written to Disney
President Richard Nunis; thanking him for the "magnani-
mous participation of Walt Disney World in this last-ditch effort to prevent the extinction of the dusky seaside sparrow.
. . . The courage and vision of Walt Disney World to invest
corporate resources and personnel in this monumental gam-
ble . . . will be recognized and appreciated throughout the

scientific and conservation community and by the public in general."

Cook and Kale had agreed to codirect the project. Although the sparrows were elderly, the codirectors had professed optimism. The *Miami Herald* reported that "the bird-lovers haven't given up. And why should they, when their drive to save the birds [was] based in Disney World, billed as a fantasy land where dreams almost always come true."

The events leading up to the transfer had been fraught with difficulty. Ellis at Santa Fe Community College had not taken kindly to the transfer of the sparrows from his care to Disney World. Although he had known all along that Kale and Fish and Wildlife were "talking" about the transfer of the sparrows, he learned of the actual decision to remove the birds from an unexpected phone call from the service. But because time was running out for the birds—and every clutch might be their last—the sparrows would be bred at Santa Fe in order not to lose the spring before their transfer. Ellis reluctantly agreed.

The hybridization had gotten off to an auspicious start. That spring Yellow mated with one of the 50 percenters from the "accidental" mating between Red and a Scott's at Florida Game and Fish several years earlier. After the hatching of the 75 percenter, Mott was quoted in the *Orlando Sentinel*, "I'm tempted to say, Eureka!" Cook, too, was elated. Ellis, who wasn't one to let optimism stand in the way of a realistic assessment, was quoted in the same article as saying, "It's cause for optimism, but not too much more. . . . For the dusky, it's basically too late. You'll never have a dusky again unless we find a female in the wild. We can never reconstitute 100 percent. Anyway you look at it, you'll always have a hybrid, not a dusky."

Ellis had been in a difficult position. To admit that anything good could come of crossbreeding would be to implicitly agree that the birds' two-year stay at Santa Fe, during which crossbreeding was forbidden, had meant loss of precious time. When Kale read the article, he was outraged at what he considered Ellis's negative attitude, and fired off a letter to him: "I'm hoping that you were misquoted, because I'm not very happy about your purported comments. It has taken a lot of time and effort on my part (and others') to convince Walt Disney World that this is a worthwhile project for a number of reasons. . . . Your quote . . . displays an ignorance about species dynamics that I would not want displayed so prominently in the press. . . . I would expect the legal-beagles of the department of interior to have such an attitude, but not someone who has had some biological training. Nature is not quite so nit-picky, fortunately, and if this project is successful we will have a biological dusky seaside sparrow regardless of whether or not it is mathematically 'pure.'"

Kale also intimated that Ellis, like Fish and Wildlife, had a racist attitude: "Even if you firmly believe in 100 percent 'purity' of the races, I should be grateful if, for the sake of this project, at least for the next several years, you refrain from publicly pouring cold water on it. If this project should be as successful as we hope it will be, Walt Disney World may well (and justifiably so) be able to realize a tremendous amount of good publicity and even a good return on their investment. But as of now, they are investing a lot of time and money into the project that really has no guaranteed promise of any success. For this alone I think they deserve our appreciation and commendation, and certainly not a belittling of the project with faulty biological opinion."

While negotiating with Fish and Wildlife to move the birds, Kale and Cook had visited Ellis, leaving him with the impression that transfer of the birds was a foregone conclusion. Ellis agreed to help design new aviaries at Discovery Island. After Kale and Cook left, Ellis called up Fish and Wildlife. Ellis then wrote to Kale: "I am at a quandary regarding this, as *one,* Fish and Wildlife advises me that *no* project has been approved or received and *two,* that I cannot see any value in our input based on a hasty evaluation of our current facilities with no knowledge of their future use. . . . At this point I am hesitant to involve our staff and facilities in recommending future dusky housing. . . . Again, unfortunately, I see us back at a point where we were two years ago with a rush to hurry into a project. The format we took has done well and protected the birds in a holding action. Now that this project is to evolve again I need to know its direction so that I can offer you our ideas."

Kale had interpreted Ellis' hesitancy as reneging on an earlier promise of cooperation, and Kale wrote back that he was "dismayed" by the letter, and couldn't help but wonder "why you have waited until now to express these feelings instead of back in July when Charlie Cook and I were visiting you. . . . Are you now suggesting that we put a brake on this project? We've already lost two years of breeding and the birds are now approaching 8–10 years of age, your sense of urgency should be increasing not diminishing . . . we don't have (and never have had) the luxury of time . . . we will [have] lost the birds long before we have the chance to breed them."

Ellis, always courteous, competent, and professional in his dealings, later offered extensive suggestions on the project proposal that Kale would send to Fish and Wildlife for approval. In time Ellis wanted nothing more than to wash his hands of the whole project. He knew that corporate biology was a complicated and often unrewarding affair. The original plans had required the aviary roof to be translucent white so enough sunlight could penetrate the cages to sustain the broomgrass. But the cages had been covered with green. Kale had told Cook the green was unacceptable. A few days later a Disney vice president had been attending a party atop the Contemporary Hotel, just across the lake from Discovery Island, and asked something to the effect of, "What is that ugly green roof?" When told, he ordered it changed, coincidentally, to white. It was clear that the sparrows would be at the whim of commercial as well as biological considerations. Said Ellis, "I sensed then where priorities lay, and I wanted nothing further to do with the project."

While Cook may have been the real thing at Disney, there was more behind the sparrow arrangement than just an altruistic effort to save an endangered species. Disney World had wanted publicity; *good* publicity. The original proposal submitted to Fish and Wildlife had contained a provision requiring that any articles to be published on the duskies be cleared through Disney World. The original proposal also had stipulated that any hybrids born at Disney World be given the scientific name *Ammospiza maritima disnei*. Fish and Wildlife rejected both ideas.

And there had been unvoiced philosophical differences between Cook and Kale from the start. Kale was a matter-of-fact scientist. Cook was an idealist who brimmed with passion and idealism; he said things like ". . . we hope the dusky will live forever." If Kale took the project as a bold scientific experiment, Cook and his employer saw it as a public relations endeavor on behalf of all endangered species—and a chance for some good publicity. Cook believed that the greatest value of the remaining males was in their poignant story being told through the vast Disney publicity apparatus. While the cages were being built on Discovery Island, Kale visited them and discovered that certain last-minute alterations had been planned—that cheaper fiberglass screening instead of aluminum screening was to be used. Kale had re-

jected the proposed change because the live-insect food—
chiefly crickets—that would be released in the cage could
chew through fiberglass. Warned Kale, "I realize that Walt
Disney World wants to keep expenses as low as possible in
this project, but the expression 'penny-wise, and pound fool-
ish' easily applies when money managers who have no knowledge of the needs and background of a project dictate design
and material. . . . This is an extremely sensitive and critical
project. People from Florida to Washington are looking over
our shoulders. . . . We will have enough problems over
which we have little or no control—we certainly don't need to
create any purposely. I hope you can get the message to the
people who make the financial decisions for this project."

Cook and Kale had known that four aging males were
about the worst scenario one could imagine. Red had died
the year before. On June 24, 1984 Blue—also known as Abraham—died of kidney failure. He was at least ten years old.
The breeding project was reduced to three aged males. With
so little hope left, some observers scoffed at the project. A
cynical curator at Chicago's Brookfield Zoo told Cook to
"turn a cat loose on the remaining birds."

Yet the first spring at Disney offered some hope. The 75
percenter hatched at Santa Fe the year before (1983) proved
to be female. In 1984 she was mated with Orange, and they
attempted to nest five times between May 2 and August 7.
She produced eight eggs, but only one of them—a male—
hatched and fledged. Cook and Kale were elated. "Eighty-
seven and a half to me is a miracle, the bird is so near
extinction," Cook told a reporter from the Associated Press.
Unfortunately, this bird was found dead in its cage with a
broken neck in early September, apparently having inadver-
tently flown into the structure. The sparrows were beginning
to inject a strong dose of reality into the Magic Kingdom.

The 50 percenter, mating with Yellow, made seven nesting attempts and produced twenty eggs, five of which hatched, but only one of these—hatched on the extremely late date of September 7—survived. The sum total of the 1984 breeding season was a single 75 percenter. Although admitting to the disappointing results, Kale was an optimist, and he looked forward to the 1985 breeding season with "great expectations." Cook, too, struggled to keep up his optimism. At the end of the 1984 breeding season, he wrote to Kale:

> Twelve months have passed since the last dusky seaside sparrows came to Discovery Island. Those months have been filled with anxiety and perhaps, at times, too great expectations of those who have tutored and built my confidence in the ultimate triumph of the "underdog."
>
> Looking back I see what a narrow gate we chose to enter and how "long the shot" we decided to take. My only regret's not having enough years to finish producing the project by virtue of the age of our subjects. However, I am hopeful, determined and thrilled that the one chick is added to the fold. Water is precious by the drop when scarce.
>
> I am looking forward, with you, to next year, and some years to come, knowing more than ever that the dusky can be regenerated by this effort. And so long as these efforts go on, we will continue to press the story for a larger audience, creating at least a small difference in the hearts and minds of some, who otherwise would have never cared.

But 1985 proved to be no better. Yellow and his 50 percent mate made six nesting attempts and laid twelve eggs, all of them infertile. White, meanwhile, who had fathered no chicks, was mated with a 25 percenter born in 1981; his mate produced eight eggs in five nesting attempts. Once again, all were infertile. Old age apparently had taken its toll. That September, on Friday the thirteenth, Yellow—heretofore the most prolific of the captives—died. As father of five of the seven hatchlings of 1984, his passing marked the loss of the most fertile male. White and Orange were to be the bearers of hope, if any was left. But White had never produced any chicks, so all rested on the shoulders of Orange. The best news of all for 1985 was that Orange and his mate—the 75 percenter sired by Yellow in 1983—produced two healthy 87 percenters during five nesting attempts and ten eggs. One was a male, one a female. One afternoon as Kale was weighing the 87 percent male, it escaped from his hand and dashed itself against an exposed water pipe in the outer enclosure, breaking its neck.

During the winter of 1986, the keeper noticed that White constantly fluffed his feathers up in an attempt to keep warm. A veterinarian came to examine him, but there was no prescription for old age. On the night of February 10, 1986, White died, reducing the dusky to a mere shadow of an existence. Only Orange remained. Despite three clutches of eggs laid by his female in 1986, all proved to be infertile. And no wonder. Orange was nearly twelve years old.

22

A Special Kind of Deprivation

When Herb Kale first visited Merritt Island in 1954 and stood beside his brother's green Chevrolet marveling at the multitude of duskies singing from the broomgrass, he could never have imagined that thirty years later the sparrow would be extinct. Kale will tell you that a special kind of personal deprivation follows the extinction of a species one has intimately known—a feeling beyond simple loss: a regret, a sadness, and an aching emptiness filled with strange and disquieting echoes.

In 1975 Kale, who was more interested in birds and conservation than in mosquitoes, left the entomology laboratory where he had worked since 1966 and went to work for the Florida Audubon Society, where today he is vice president of Ornithology. It was in his office at the society's headquarters, then in Maitland, a suburb of Orlando, that I first met Herb Kale in 1987. Kale's office was an avalanche of papers and publications, specimen jars, books, and assorted paraphernalia. I had spoken with him on numerous occasions by telephone, and he never failed to apologize for speaking in a soft, raspy voice. In the 1960s he had developed laryngeal papillomas, a benign warty growth of the vocal chords. Surgical treatment left scars that affected his voice.

After apologizing for his soft voice and for the ransacked condition of his office, he invited me to look around. Two mounted bird specimens—a fulvous whistling duck and an American kestrel—were balanced on a mound of papers atop a shelf that stood on a table in the middle of the office. The walls were lined with steel and wood bookshelves holding a collection of bird books far superior to most university libraries I have seen. In the left corner stood a high and narrow shelf with dozens of formalin-filled jars containing various embryos, bird gizzards, and other specimens. His own desk, just inside the door, may have been wooden or metal; one couldn't tell for all the correspondence scattered across its top. Lithographs and photographs hung, some slightly off kilter, on all the available wall space. In the back right corner of his office, balanced on a four-door file cabinet, stood a tall clump of dried broomgrass, and tucked at its base was a neat, circular, exquisitely woven dusky nest with a near-perfect symmetry. Kale sat back in his swivel chair. The dusky was still a painful subject for him:

"A lot of people have never heard of the dusky, although in the 1950s and 1960s it was quite a famous bird because its rarity made it popular among birders. People traveled from all over the country to Merritt Island just so they could get a glimpse of it and add it to their life list. Birders had traditionally been the dusky's strongest constituency. They formed the backbone of powerful conservation groups such as the Audubon Society and the American Birding Association. These supporters were among the dusky's most powerful allies, because they were very vocal, always writing to their congressmen. But for too many bird-watchers, their support was built upon a compulsion to collect names of species, not to protect birds or their habitat. In 1973, just as the sparrow was gaining political recognition with the Endangered Species Acts, it lost the support of the bird-watching community almost overnight. The ornithologist's bible is the *Checklist of North American Birds*. Every so often a new edition comes out that incorporates the ever-changing taxonomy of birds—what is a species, subspecies, and what have you. Prior to 1973, the *Checklist* considered the dusky a species. But a supplement to the fifth edition, published that year, demoted the sparrow to a subspecies, and subspecies do not count on your life list of birds. The thousands of birders no longer came to Merritt Island to see the dusky, because as a subspecies, it no longer counted as a "life" bird. With the loss of the huge birding constituency, the political clout to promote the sparrow was lost. People stopped calling my office to inquire about it. No one wanted to see it anymore."

A life-long birder, Kale was saddened by the sudden loss of interest. Many birders, he realized, were not so much supporters as collectors. Many birders are often not so much lovers of birds, as lovers of lists. It is a fraternity of highly competitive individuals who, if they had not been devoted to birds, might have been just as happy collecting postage stamps.

Kale also told me another story, that while humorous to some, struck him as a sad and perverse commentary on the way some people felt about endangered species. On May 26, 1977, a landowner near Merritt Island received a letter, on stationery bearing the heading of Division of Fisheries and Wildlife, Commonwealth of Massachusetts, stating that the Massachusetts Ornithological Society had established a laboratory at Plum Island, Massachusetts, and hoped to collect dusky eggs—six of which were in a nest on his property—for captive breeding purposes. The letter requested "permission to trespass upon [your] property and remove eggs from the nest. . . . For each egg we remove from the nest, we are prepared to pay the sum of $500.00."

Kale ended up with a copy of the letter and immediately sent it on to the executive director of the Massachusetts Audubon Society. "We do not know whether this is a hoax or what," Kale wrote. "A copy of this strange letter has also been given to the law enforcement division of the Fish and Wildlife Service."

About a week later, Kale received a reply from Massachusetts Audubon, stating that the letter, indeed, had been a hoax: "It appears that a month or so ago, some gal wandered into the division offices and struck up a conversation with the secretary (who was new on the job) and asked for a sheet of official stationery and an envelope. She said that her father wanted to play a practical joke—amazingly enough, the girl gave her the stationery. . . . I suggested to the division that they ask for an opinion from the Attorney General's office on what laws were violated by the use of official stationery."

Then Kale's telephone rang. He chatted for a moment then hung up and began digging through a mound of scattered papers on his desk. He pulled out a white cardboard box, from which he drew out a small bottle, and held it up to the diffuse light. "Here's Yellow," Kale said. Yellow, among the last captive duskies, had passed away in 1985. "I'm mailing him off to the Smithsonian, in Washington, tomorrow. That will be his permanent resting place, among all the other extinct animals there."

I held the bottle and rotated it against the light. Thin white membranous lids covered the little eyes. The bright yellow marking above the eyes and on the wings' edges were still visible. First soaked in formalin, then stored in alcohol, the bird had retained its vivid colors. I placed the bottle on the windowsill and got a good back-lit photograph of it. Today a five-by-seven-inch print from the slide stands on my bookcase, next to framed Polaroid shots of the *Apollo 11* lift-off I had witnessed almost twenty years earlier.

Kale and I talked for two hours. He reminisced about his own trip to Merritt Island in 1954 and the abundance of sparrows he saw. He spoke wearily until the subject of the Beeline came up. Then his animation returned: "They lied to us about the course of the highway! They lied about the borrow pit! Once the road was in place, it was only a matter of time before developers came in. Ask anybody at Port St. Johns and Canaveral Groves if they've even heard of the dusky! The Beeline is built on Big Colony!"

Kale drew a deep breath. The subject of the dusky was depressing him.

23

Eternal Moment

Orange gained near celebrity status during his tenure at Disney World. Newspapers and magazines around the country published stories about him. Like an elderly states-man in his final days, Orange came to be described less as a living figure and more in eulogistic tones. His actual pres-ence would pale compared to the anticipated historical legacy he would leave behind. A recap of Orange's life might have read like this: Orange began his public career on July 25, 1978, when he was netted and banded in the wild, north of State Road 50, in Brevard County, Florida. In 1980, he was again netted seven or eight miles south, unexpectedly, in the fork of the Beeline Expressway and sent in a sack to captivity at the Florida Game and Fresh Water Fish Commission in Gainesville. On April 20, 1981, on orders of Fish and Wildlife, Orange was transferred to aviaries at the Santa Fe Community College Teaching Zoo, where he resided for the next two years. In September of 1983 he was authorized to

be part of a crossbreeding program at Disney World and sent
to Orlando. There he fathered a generation of part-duskies,
producing an 87 percenter in 1984, and several more in
1985. Once he came down with a severe eye infection but,
after treatment with an antibiotic, recovered, though was left
partially blind. Orange produced three infertile clutches of
eggs in 1986. Cook described the aging Orange as "middle-
aged-looking, chubby, a little slower and less sure in his landings."

Throughout his ordeal as a captive bird, where others
had grown more or less accustomed to people, Orange remained shy and solitary, if curious. Unlike the more outgo-
ing Abraham, for example, Orange usually remained hidden
in the broomgrass of his cage. He never sang naturally, as
there were no other duskies to cause him to defend a territory. This is what Cook and his keeper noticed most. Only
when they brought the same minute-long tape that he had
heard hundreds of time before, was Orange coaxed into
song.

At twelve years old, Orange was perhaps the longest-lived
dusky ever, but as winter of 1986 bloomed into spring of
1987, it dawned on Cook that even this sparrow would not
live forever. And when he died, so would the entire dusky
race. Cook collected some final video pictures of Orange for
posterity. Kale told Cook to keep some dry ice handy.

At about 4:30 P.M. on June 12, 1987, senior keeper Danforth went to check on Orange and the remaining hybrids.
Orange seemed perky—so it was noted in the logbook she
kept. She ran fresh water through the "ponds" and fed him
wax worms and crickets. Orange sang loudly in response to
recordings played to him that day. Over the next two days,
all seemed well with the sparrow.

Sometime on the night of June 15 or early on June 16,
1987, surrounded by the phantasmagoria of Disney World,

Orange huddled on the sandy ground beneath the broom-grass and died. When Danforth arrived on Discovery Island early on the morning of June 16 and went to the aviaries, she noticed the cage to be unusually quiet. When she looked closer, she found Orange, lying on his right side by the pond, his wings slightly spread as if in a final attempt to keep from falling over. She fought off her emotions and tried to put into place the protocol. But first she picked him up and held him quietly in both her hands. An assistant keeper was feeding fruit to the toucans nearby. With the body of Orange in her hands, Lisa walked over to her and said, "This is the last bird, he's dead." Still cradling Orange in her shaking palms, Danforth walked silently to the backstage area of Discovery Island. She pulled a Ziploc baggy from a cabinet and slipped Orange's body into it, then placed him in an empty refrigerator. She didn't know exactly what to tell Cook, so she stood for a while thinking about it. Then she called him at home—he was just getting ready for work—greeted him cheerfully as if nothing had happened, then blurted out: "Charlie, Orange is in a Ziploc bag in the refrigerator."

Cook paused, then said, "I'll be right there."

When Cook arrived he took Orange from the refrigerator, removed him from the bag, and put the chilled body on the counter. As the protocol dictated, Cook carefully cut him open and removed some tissues. He packed the specimens in the dry ice and sent them Federal Express to a geneticist at the University of Georgia for genetic analysis. Others would go to a pathologist to determine the cause of death. Cook called Kale: "He's gone, Herb. Orange is dead."

The formalities completed, Cook stopped to think about what had happened. From that moment on, his life would be different. He later explained, "It was like watching a comet fade. I just cried when they were gone because no matter what I did, there could never be more duskies. I had rushes of memory—driving the birds from Gainesville, their singing in the aviaries in spring and summer, their small nests tucked in the broomgrass. The aviaries went silent. Orange took the last dusky seaside sparrow song on earth with him."

Brian Sharp was twenty-four years old when he came to Merritt Island; he was forty-three when the last dusky died. And the now gray-haired biologist all but wept when he heard the news. He wrote an epitaph to the dusky and to the land where it had once lived. It went, in part:

Imagine central Florida in springtime . . . before there was Disney World and Cape Canaveral, before rocket launchings and shuttle disasters. . . . The grassland is enclosed in a morning mist—there is no horizon. The ghostly outlines of palm trees are suspended in an atmosphere of gray softness. Nightbirds, black rails, are calling yet, *kiskadee, kiskadee.* Off-stage a chuck-will's-widow lapses into silence, last murmurs of the night.

In the top of a tussock of grass, on its sunward side, a dark shape, a small bird, feathers wet with dew, sits quietly, observant, incorporating the sun's early warmth. Nearby, there is a faint and tentative song, and the sound is reabsorbed into the morning quiet. . . . There are courtship displays accompanied by sweet, softer, intimate notes. And mounting songflights into the air, expressions of superexuberance. . . . While all around the salt-grass meadow, dotted with palm trees and pointillist with pink and yellow, stretched lime-green and vibrant to the far horizon. . . .

It has been suggested that you might not be missed. To think that a necklace would never miss one of its pearls, or a song one of its notes. Neither this spring, nor ever again, will your exuberant performances appear on nature's stage. Your passing is a measure of our own inordinate and perhaps temporary success as a species. But our progress is also our loss. Your loss is our world and ourselves diminished. And except perhaps for this account of the days of your prosperity, of the extent of our impoverishment we will hardly even have been aware. Now, then, let us depart in peace.

Sharp sent the epitaph to some friends. Kale, upon receiving reading it, wrote back: "Being the trained scientist and objective observer of the world that I am, I was being strong and stalwart, cool and calm. When it died, people phoned or wrote condolences, as if the bird were actually mine, and asked, 'Aren't you sad?' I replied, 'Yes, a little, but it was inevitable, we were expecting it.' Not a tear or even a near-tear. After all, I'm a scientist, not one of those emotional conservationists. Then came your manuscript. . . . I broke down and cried and cried. . . . I'll never, never again see that bird or hear that song in the St. Johns marshes."

Sharp also sent a copy to his former wife Kathi. She wrote back, "Probably you more than anyone else know the greatest sense of loss having known the dusky and the place it lived so intimately and appreciatively. . . . It is one of the saddest things I have ever known, the death of the dusky, and your paper is something I will always treasure. . . . I know I'll never forget it, nor you either."

24

Broken Images

I made my final two trips to Brevard County in 1989 and 1990. Jack Salmela had retired as manager of the Brevard Country Mosquito Control District in 1986 to be with his wife Helen, who was dying of breast cancer. Two years later, after forty-four years of marriage, she passed away. Salmela's life seemed to have lost its luster just as it should have reached its peak. He was baffled by the rising condemnation of the world that, a decade earlier, had made him something of a local hero for his mosquito-fighting efforts.

After his wife's death, with memories of his fallen son Bobby still fresh in his mind, Salmela was a broken man, too despondent to even answer the phone at home. His daughter Joy came home and found him so depressed that she called her old admirer Chuck Trost in Idaho and asked him to please write to her father with an encouraging word. Trost, of course, did, for although they had lost contact over the years, he still loved Salmela.

Salmela soon remarried, and while keeping his own home in Melbourne, settled into his new wife's comfortable house on the main highway through Sebastian. It was only a few blocks from where my own father had grown up. On one of my final trips, I paid Salmela a call. I sat in the lounge chair, and his wife Betty brought us tall glasses of amber iced tea. Salmela was eager to make sure I understood the efforts Mosquito Control had made on behalf of the dusky. He showed me an award he had won shortly before his retirement—the Conservation Service Award of the Department of the Interior—the highest private honor, he explained, bestowed by the secretary of the interior on a private citizen. The accompanying citation, signed by Secretary Donald P. Hodel, praised Salmela for prompting "efforts by State and local Audubon Societies in Florida and the Fish and Wildlife to begin active management to halt the decline of the dusky seashore [sic] sparrow. . . . In 1963 through 1965, and again in 1968, he arranged for the use of helicopters by Fish and Wildlife Service biologists in conducting extensive aerial surveys of refuge lands." As I read the citation he intoned, "Gosh, I would never have imagined twenty years ago that the little sparrow would be extinct."

Salmela never accepted that Mosquito Control alone was responsible for the decline of the dusky, as if the bird's disappearance was epiphenomenal. In one of his last letters as director of Mosquito Control, he had written to an authority on mosquito control at Rutgers University, who had requested information about the dusky:

> . . . unless you are quite knowledgeable of [the dusky's] range you would be led to believe that mosquito control is solely responsible for its demise. In spite of the tremendous benefit received from our source reduction work in the salt-marsh on Merritt Island, it is true that we altered the habitat to the detriment of the dusky. However, you will see that mosquito

control became concerned at an early date and three areas were managed separately for the dusky. But our efforts were evidently in vain, and the question is: Why? I have my own opinion, but no scientific basis for support.

Instead of condemning mosquito control for its work on Merritt Island, it would be better to study the problem in the St. Johns marsh where a large number of duskies were present. . . . The decline of the dusky in this vast area was even more dramatic, and mosquito control played no part except to show them where they were.

In his opinion, the incessant study of the bird on Merritt Island had contributed to the decline. "Just as the opened dikes offered the dusky a chance to recover, nearly every sparrow surviving on the island was trapped and banded during breeding season, when they were probably most sensitive to interruption," he said. "You have to wonder what impact studies had on the bird. Not many birds will tolerate the kind of intrusion the dusky was subjected to. They just don't like people being around them all the time. In the end, the poor old dusky didn't have much privacy."

Then Salmela, as if trying to escape the weight of a controversy he neither wanted nor expected, spoke wistfully about the old times in Sebastian. He told me how, as a youngster, he fished in the shallow backwaters of the Sebastian Inlet, where the Indian River sweeps between two long rock jetties of great black, algae-slick, barnacle-encrusted boulders before emptying into the Atlantic. I explained to him that my father had actually built the jetties in the 1950s. We, too, fished there, and it was a rare day my father and I returned without red snapper, sleek snook, or pompano the color of a harvest moon. Salmela told me about an acquaintance he used to fish with.

"We called him 'Scrap'," he said.

"'Scrap' Walters?" I asked.

"Yes," he replied.

"That was my father," I said, startled. Salmela seemed as surprised as I was.

There seemed to be a lesson in that unexpected revelation. Somehow it personally implicated me. When I was a child, we heralded the mosquito truck as it rolled down the narrow street behind our house. We ran behind it, inhaling the sweet aroma of the DDT spewing from its nozzles. It came down the narrow streets behind our house because Jack Salmela had ordered it to.

Salmela suggested we take a ride through Sebastian. Along the river, sailboat mains luffed like white moths trapped on water. We drove down Main Street, and Salmela said, "Look over there!" There stood an old rectangular metal-sided garage. Barely visible on the side in faded black block letters was the name Walters. Many years ago, my grandfather owned the garage.

Later that day I bid farewell to Salmela and drove up to Maitland, where I stopped by to see Kale at the Audubon House. I asked him the whereabouts of Orange's remains. Kale seemed to almost wince when I asked, then put on his detached face and led me quietly downstairs and into a back room. A freezer sat in one corner. He opened it, shuffled through the stiff bodies of some plastic-wrapped specimens, finally came across the Ziploc plastic bag. Kale lifted his head out of the clouds of frost and held up the baggy containing a small aluminum-foil-wrapped package.

"Here he is!"

I undid the twist at the top, slowly unwrapped the foil, and folded back the soft cotton gauze enshrouding the dead sparrow. He looked in fine shape for a dead bird, the body scarcely showing the scars from tissues that had been removed and sent to various laboratories—intestine, heart, part of his thigh bone, a little tibia, and his two testes. Kale said that Orange, rendered vulnerable by his old age, had died from a fungal infection, which had targeted one of Orange's testes, then spread throughout his body.

I must have stood there holding Orange for a long time. Would the world ever miss a thing so small, a race so limited? I recalled Kale's vivid descriptions of his first visit to the Merritt Island marsh nearly forty years before, when the birds were singing everywhere around him. I thought of Sharp's triumphant discovery of Big Colony, and of the last sparrows in the refuge north of State Road 50, where Orange himself had lived. Kale let me hold Orange for as long as I wanted, and not until my hand became wet with melting ice crystals did it occur to me that Orange was thawing out. I rewrapped him carefully, put him back in the bag, and lowered him between the frosted walls of the freezer. Kale said Orange would be sent to the Smithsonian for final keeping. We distracted ourselves with small talk, then returned to Kale's office.

As we walked up the stairs, an announcement from the secretary downstairs over the loudspeaker said that a Boeing 747 with the space shuttle *Columbia* piggybacked on the fuselage was passing over Maitland toward the Kennedy Space Center, bringing the shuttle back to Florida from California, where it had landed several days before after a successful mission into space. We ran outside and watched through squinting eyes as the mated machines descended through a light layer of clouds, arcing down toward the shuttle landing strip.

Next day I drove along the county's coastal highway, threading the narrow sand spit stretching from the southern tip of Cape Canaveral. The Indian River was a quarter of a mile off to my right, the Atlantic Ocean less than a hundred yards off to my left. But nowhere could I see either the river or ocean. Motels have cannibalized the view. Along residential sections of the highway, peeling garage doors are backed up to within five yards of the highway. I continued past Satellite Beach until I came to the small white-on-green highway sign marking the boundary of Canova Beach. I parked the car in a Hilton lot and climbed across a dune. Twenty-five years ago a long enclosed pier there stood on towering fir pilings as it jutted from the bulkhead of sea-grape-smothered sand dunes and into the roiling surf. On Sundays my father, a couple of my brothers, and I often rode up to Canova's Pier to inspect the leathery dumb-faced sharks that proud fishermen hung from the sea-worn crossbeams beneath the pier. I had often sat at the mahogany snack bar in the covered pier drinking orange juice while my father traded stories with the proprietor, Carlos Canova, a menagerie of tatoos leaping from beneath the neck and sleeves of his white T-shirt, down his arms and over his elbows, devouring in bright and violent detail the back of both hands. The pier had since become dilapidated and had blown down in a hurricane. The whole stretch of beach was hotels now, with spacious balconies overlooking the ocean. It was gratifying to see that at least old man Canova's name was still remembered on a reflective highway sign, because everything else had disappeared.

I drove a little farther south and pulled into the parking lot of a Holiday Inn overlooking the beach, and I got out. Where the asphalt lot gave way to the rippled edge of a dune tufted in sea oats and hung with rubbery round leaves of sea grapes, stood the foundation of an old dwelling. A small porch of cement slabs, with a perimeter formed by a single layer of cinderblocks retaining a trace of their original paint, jutted from the foundation into the dune, and on the opposite side of the rectangular foundation, three narrow stairs. It was the footing of the Merrimac Bar. The pines that once separated it from the beach house were gone and so was almost everything else.

About thirty yards away, just where our beach house had

missile I was watching was miles off the Cape. The projectile rose vertically, then seemed to explode in a celebratory cascade of orange fires streaming down like the burning tentacles of a roman candle. I made a note of the date and time, expecting I could find out what it was later on. That evening I drove along I-95 toward the Jacksonville airport and heard on the news over the car radio that a test missile, launched from a Titan submarine that morning miles off Cape Canaveral, had exploded along its misdirected path and fallen back into the sea. I thought: Just like that, shoot for the stars and wind up in the soup where life began.

Epilogue

O ne might have hoped that if the dusky's story had to end so tragically, it might have ended with the death of Orange. It did not. Some of Orange's genes still lived on in the hybrids born at Santa Fe and Disney World: one 87 percenter, one 50 percenter, and two 75 percenters. Neither full dusky nor full Scott's, these hybrids inhabited a genetic limbo. No one called Herb Kale to ask about them. With the death of Orange in 1987, reporters no longer kept vigil over Discovery Island. The hybrids were a reminder of a failed mission to save the dusky seaside sparrow.

Then came another blow to the stragglers. In February, 1989, geneticists at the University of Georgia, Athens, who had been sent some of Orange's tissue, concluded that Orange was genetically virtually indistinguishable from the still common variety of seaside sparrow that lived along the Atlantic coast. Of course, this was merely a confirmation of what Kale, Hardy, and others had suspected all along—that the dusky was merely a subtle variation on a theme. Then, in a reach for political relevance, the geneticists implied that the exceptional rescue efforts for the dusky had been misdirected. Cook and many others involved in the dusky project took the news hard.

But the story of the hybrids was not over. On June 15, 1989, Lisanne Renner, a reporter for the *Orlando Sentinel* received an anonymous tip. According to the caller, earlier that year, on March 27, a storm struck Discovery Island, damaging the aviary and either freeing or killing the four remaining hybrid duskies. The caller said that the next morning a keeper found one bird dead in the damaged cage; a second remained in the cage but escaped when the keepers tried to move it. The other two birds were not accounted for. According to the article published in the *Orlando Sentinel* on June 16—the second anniversary of Orange's death—"One theory is that rodents ate the two birds, though there is no evidence of that. Another theory is that the scared birds pushed their way through flimsy screening and flew through the hole in the fiberglass roof. Disney planned to refurbish the cage this year." In the article Cook was quoted as describing the loss "a devastating event."

But the explanation that a storm had claimed the hybrids was far more complex than at first it seemed. In a detailed letter, Kale explained it to me this way: On May 31, 1989, about two weeks before the anonymous tip, Cook had informed him that all the hybrids were "dead or lost." Cook explained that rats had gotten into the cages and killed two of them and that, on March 27, the remaining birds had been "released for their own safety." Stunned and angry that Cook had waited so long to tell him, Kale told Cook that the release was a "death penalty" for the birds. For his part, Cook had neither the heart nor the nerve to tell him earlier.

The next day, on June 1, Kale went to Discovery Island.

Cook was unavailable, but one of the caretakers of the hybrids told Kale that rats had probably entered the aviary through holes in the roof. (The holes had been present for several months.) Like the roofs, the screen for the inner cage had also fallen into disrepair, enabling the rats to squeeze in. The caretaker told Kale that a surviving hybrid—the 75 percent female—had been released accidentally when an inexperienced worker tried to move it to safer quarters. It lived on the island for about three weeks before disappearing. When Kale examined the cages during the visit, he found primary feathers and a few scattered body feathers in two of the cages—telltale signs of rat predation.

Kale then told Cook that Walt Disney World was going to have to inform the press. According to Kale's letter to me, Cook replied that "he would tell the press that a storm broke the cages and the birds escaped." Some of Kale's colleagues at the Florida Audubon Society felt that the truth should be revealed, but Kale decided that this would only get Cook in trouble with his superiors and "nothing positive would come of it." Similarly, when the reporter from the *Orlando Sentinel* called Kale to ask his opinion on the anonymous tip and the storm theory, he avoided the issue and said, ". . . what else can we do but accept [the statements] in good faith."

In fact, long before Kale wrote to me detailing the fate of the last hybrids, I had visited Discovery Island to speak with Lisa Danforth about the last days of Orange. Much had changed since my earlier visits. Cook had been transferred to another job at Disney World after officials from Florida Game and Fresh Water Fish Commission discovered irregularities concerning state permits for keeping wildlife on the island and were investigating various other charges. When I arrived, Disney manager Keven Myers told me that I could speak with Danforth only if he or another manager were present; that I must not ask *any* questions about the hybrids. But

I did manage to speak with some employees confidentially about the hybrids. I was told that the storm story had indeed been fabricated to conceal the fate of the hybrids. Just to make doubly sure, I did some investigating on my own.

I called the National Climactic Data Center in Asheville, North Carolina, which keeps daily weather records for the United States. After consulting the records, meteorologist Alex Graumann told me that during the period on and around March 27, 1989, ". . . there were seven days of dry weather. The last rain was on March 23; another rain shower occurred on March 31. On March 27 [the day of the alleged storm] it was 86 degrees in Orlando, 12 degrees above normal, with partly to mostly sunny conditions. It was great vacation weather."

I then ordered weather-radar records of the county to see if a localized storm might have passed through. They would show nearly all weather activity in the area. The records showed no storm activity in the Orlando area—in fact, nothing remotely resembling a real storm in all northern Florida.

So Kale's letter, which arrived only days before this book went to press, confirmed what by then had already become apparent: the storm story was meant to cover up the fact that the hybrids had died not by an act of God, but out of neglect by their earthly keepers.

Unfortunately, this was not the end of the saga. I had been told that the only complete written record of the hybrids' tenure on Discovery Island were special logbooks that Danforth and others on the island had maintained. Daily entries included descriptions of the deteriorating aviaries and behavioral observations, and presumably they chronicled the fate of the birds. But more important, these logs were an invaluable record of the remaining years of the last dusky seaside sparrows in existence, as well. Kale had recorded the weights of the sparrows in them, and keepers recorded many of their behavioral observations. There was probably nothing quite like these books; they were a unique and detailed record of the last years of an extinct animal. They also held clues, it seemed, to the fate of the last hybrids.

After learning of the existence of these documents, I asked Myers as well as the supervisor of operations on Discovery Island, Bill Gillett, if I could see the logs. Both told me that the books had "disappeared." They believed that agents of the Florida Game and Fresh Water Fish Commission had confiscated the books during a raid of the island in connection with the permitting irregularities and other charges. But when I wrote to Lt. John L. Moran, who headed the investigation, about the dusky logs, he replied in a letter of August 9, 1990, "Apparently you have received some erroneous information about the records. . . . Neither the Florida Game and Fresh Water Fish Commission nor the U.S. Fish and Wildlife Service seized any records pertaining to the sparrows." Subsequently I made repeated requests to Disney management concerning the dusky logs, finally eliciting a curt note: "We are sorry to inform you that the dusky seaside sparrow logbooks are not available." Gillett later added, "They must be in a deep vault somewhere." Later I met privately with Cook in the lobby of the Hyatt Hotel near Disney World. He said he didn't know where the logs were either but was confident he would find them. Almost two years later, he still had not done so.

What has become of the dusky logs? One can only hope that they have not been destroyed and that they will resurface again, for there now seems little to be gained if they are being concealed. Like the duskies, the logs were entrusted to Disney World in an act of faith. And like the sparrows, the books belonged to everyone. They were not Disney's to lose and certainly not theirs to conceal.

Despite the initial efforts on behalf of the sparrows, the

specter of the logs' disappearance will haunt Walt Disney World as long as the books are gone, for in their absence each generation will fill the void with a parable of faith betrayed, each lending an angry voice to the tragic loss not only of the birds, but of the knowledge and memory of their stay on Discovery Island.

So it was that the dusky seaside sparrow became extinct and that the written account of its last days on earth was taken from us all.

Postscript: On December 12, 1990, the U.S. Fish and Wildlife Service officially declared the dusky seaside sparrow extinct, and its name was removed from the federal register list of endangered species.

Notes

Quote

Page vii: T. S. Eliot, *The Waste Land and Other Poems* (New York: Harcourt Brace Jovanovich, 1979).

Acknowledgments

Page ix: "The essential matter of history . . . ": Frederic Maitland, quoted in "Notebook," *Harper's*, January 1990, p. 8.

Prologue

Page xiv: 475 species of birds: Florida Game and Fresh Water Fish Commission, *A Checklist of Florida's Birds*.

Page xiv: 3000 native plant species: Fleming et al.

Page xiv: species of reptiles and amphibians: Florida Game and Fresh Water Fish Commission, *A Checklist of Florida's Amphibians and Reptiles*.

Page xiv: 94 species of wild mammals: Florida Game and Fresh Water Fish Commission, *A Checklist of Florida's Mammals*.

Page xv: Eucharistic ritual: MacKinnon and Baldanza, p. 26.

Page xv: "magnificent desolation": Wilford, p. 269.

Page xv: "greatest week in the history of the world since creation": Ibid., p. 285.

Page xvi: carried on live television around the world: NASA, *The Kennedy Space Center Story.*

1 An Island Between Two Rivers

Page 1: loggerhead sea turtles: About 95 percent of the turtles nesting along the beach at Merritt Island are loggerheads. A few green sea turtles and leatherbacks also nest there.

Page 4: "canebearer": Gill and Read, eds., p. 107.

Page 5: ". . . low and far away, and drops from view": Federal Writers' Project, p. 345.

Page 5: C. T. Simpson: Ibid., p. 346.

Page 6: tough leaves of a Mediterranean species: Teal, p. 84.

Page 6: seventy days a year: Sharp, "Conservation of the Dusky Seaside Sparrow," pp. 175–76.

Page 6: the cycles of . . . salt marsh: Teal, pp. 84–101.

Page 6: *Spartina*, also known as broomgrass: Jack Salmela, personal communication; *Spartina* is also commonly called cordgrass, but most Brevard County natives refer to S. *Bakeri* as broomgrass.

Page 6: two and a half miles wide: The marsh ranged from from 0.8 to 4 kilometers across. Sykes.

Page 7: oxygen-breathing microorganisms: Teal.

Page 7: salt hay: *Distichlis spicata.*

Page 7: black needle rush: *Juncus roemerianus.*

Page 7: glasswort: Leenhouts and Baker. Two types of glasswort grew in the marsh, annual glasswort, *Salicornia bigelovii*, and perennial glasswort, *Salicornia virginica.* Teal, p. 109. The *Salicornia* go by a number of common names, including chicken toe, saltwort, pickle plant, and marsh sapphire.

Page 8: seaoxeye: *Borrichia frutescens.*

Page 8: groundsel-tree: *Baccharis halimifolia.*

Page 8: last black bear: Several months before his death, Johnny Johnson, a local historian and ornithologist with the Brevard County Museum, told me that he had "run a bear off the island" in 1951. He said a Titusville newspaper account saying that the last bear was shot on the island that same year is probably correct.

Page 9: endangered or threatened species . . . inhabit Merritt Island: As of early 1992, Merritt Island National Wildlife Refuge.

Notes

Page 9: International Council for Bird Preservation (ICBP): Washington, D.C.

Page 9: Starlings . . . among the few species that continue to increase: Terborgh, *Where Have All the Duskies Gone? Essays on the Biology and Conservation of Birds That Migrate to the American Tropics* (Princeton, NJ: Princeton University Press, 1991).

Page 9: Merritt Island . . . hosted a diversity of species: The specific types of shearwaters, petrels, herons, egrets, ducks, and other birds found on Merritt Island can be found in "Birds: Merritt Island National Wildlife Refuge," a checklist published by the Merritt Island National Wildlife Refuge.

Page 9: 1875 a Florida guide writer: Rambler.

Page 10: ducks . . . thrashing their web feet against the water: Lon Ellis, personal communication.

Page 10: numbers today are in steep decline: Dwight Cooley, biologist, Merritt Island National Wildlife Refuge, personal communication.

Page 10: red-pouched magnificent frigate birds: Dwight Cooley, personal communication.

Page 10: the clapper rails and the seaside sparrows: Quay, p. 2.

2 The Sparrow

Page 11: they drove across a causeway: The road Kale used was built in the late 1920s (the first permanent alteration to the marsh on Merritt Island) and remained unpaved until 1942. Today it is State Road 402.

Page 12: *Checklist of North American Birds*: American Ornithologists' Union, 1957.

Page 14: ". . . zig-zag notes similar . . . to the song of the marsh wrens": Nicholson, "Nesting Habits of Seaside Sparrows," p. 229.

Page 14: during the late Jurassic period . . . 150 million years ago: Raven and Johnson, p. 457.

Page 15: Potential predators included . . . snakes: U.S. Fish and Wildlife Service, "The Dusky Seaside Sparrow." The main predacious snakes were *Lampropeltis getulus* and *Agkistrodon piscivorous*.

Page 15: ants . . . forced adults to abandon their nests: Ibid.

Page 15: feed a fledgling an inch-long green worm: Nicholson, "Nesting Habits of Seaside Sparrows," p. 230.

Page 16: —a distance that would . . . increase over the . . . years of the dusky's decline: U.S. Fish and Wildlife Service, "The Dusky Seaside Sparrow."

Page 16: ". . . so deftly and craftily was this done": Nicholson, "Nesting Habits of Seaside Sparrows," p. 232.

Page 16: *Birds of Eastern North America*: Revised edition published in 1934. Chapman's account described an abundance of duskies on the island, but ended with the phrase "Nest and eggs unknown." Fueled by this secret, over the next three years egg collector O. E. Baynard became obsessed with finding a dusky nest. He wrote, "A bird whose range covered only a few square miles, and whose nest had never been found, was a 'slam' on the ability of us true Oologists." In failing health, Baynard set out with a friend into a gale, but found no nests. They later went out and dragged a rope across the marsh until they flushed a dusky, walked a short ways and discovered a nest with three eggs. Wrote Baynard, "To say that we were elated is expressing it mildly and we did a regular Indian Tango or some other kind of dance. . . . Returning to our boat near dusk we laid our plans for the next day and vowed we would find more nests or never leave the spot." (Baynard, 1914). No laws at the time prohibited the collecting of duskies or their nests.

3 Apollo on the Moon

Page 18: Fulgencio Batista y Zaldivar: Lon Ellis, personal communication.

Page 19: NASA had paid $72 million for about 140,000 acres: Bensen and Faherty, p. 107.

Page 19: from the Indian River in the west to the Atlantic Ocean and Cape Canaveral in the east: Dick Young, Public Affairs, NASA, personal communication.

Page 19: 2500 acres of citrus groves: Bensen and Faherty.

Page 20: relatives to visit the other: Ibid., pp. 96–98.

Page 20: Records indicate . . . duskies . . . historically nested along the western area of the Cape: There is some debate about just how far onto the Cape the duskies ranged. My information on historical distribution is based on Sykes, "Decline and Disappearance of the Dusky Seaside Sparrow"; and Sykes, personal communication.

Page 20: These early incursions had a minimal impact on the dusky: Trost, "Dusky Seaside Sparrow."

Page 20: DDT . . . eliminated up to 70 percent of the duskies in the vicinity of Merritt Island between 1942 to 1953: Ibid.

Page 20: nudist colony: Lon Ellis, personal communication.

Page 21:—engineers connected large copper grounding wires to the pilings: Bensen and Faherty, p. 254.

Page 21: A structure rising 526 feet high: NASA, *The Kennedy Space Center*, p. 20.

Page 22: —almost the equivalent of the Pentagon: Ibid., p. 17.

Page 22: Its bay door would be taller than the Statue of Liberty: Ibid., p. 22.

Page 22: ". . . a lot of hay in there.": Ibid., p. 17.

Page 22: A network of roads . . . was built through several areas of dusky habitat: Based on Sykes's ("Decline and Disappearance of the Dusky Seaside Sparrow") depiction of the historical distribution of the dusky, the roads NASA built connecting the series of launch pads along the Cape skirted dusky habitat along the east side of the Banana River. The railroad connecting Launchpad 40 and 41 also cut directly through former dusky habitat.

Page 22-24: The archaeology of Merritt Island is covered thoroughly in Ehrenhard, "Canaveral National Seashore"; Griffin and Miller, "Cultural Resource Reconnaisance"; Levey et al., "An Archaelogical Survey"; Long, "Antiquities Resources"; and Martinez, "Cultural Resource Assessment."

Page 24: Albert J. Treib: Bensen and Faherty, p. 770.

Page 25: *Handbook of Mosquito Control for Florida*: Bureau of Entomology, 1974.

Page 26: The insects . . . extinguished the lanterns used by fishermen who came to the island: NASA, *Spaceport News*, p. 4.

Page 26: 500 landings per minute: Ibid.

Page 26: "When mosquitoes die they go to Merritt Island; when they get hungry they come to Titusville": My father used this phrase.

Page 26: "land of swamps, of quagmire, of frogs and alligators and mosquitoes": Ibid.

Page 27: Brevard County was the first place in the world where resistance of saltwater mosquitoes to DDT was documented: At the "Hearings on Estuarine Pollution and Its Control," held in Orlando on March 12, 1968, Maurice Provost stated, ". . . the first evidence in the world . . . of mosquito resistance to DDT appeared in the salt-marsh mosquitoes of Brevard County." He cites *Journal of Economic Entomology* 43(4):506.

Page 27: the air force and Brevard County would join forces in the eradication effort: Bensen and Faherty, p. 251.

Page 29: transient specialists moved in: Ibid., p. 309.

Page 29: ". . . leading to the development of ulcers": Ibid. Of course, the connection between stress and the increasing incidence of ulcers in children is circumstantial. Other factors cannot be ruled out—including the physical effects of DDT.

Page 29: Divorce rates also soared: Ibid., pp. 314-15.

Page 30: the bureaucratic ancestor of the U.S. Fish and Wildlife Service: At the time, this was the Bureau of Sports Fisheries and Wildlife. In 1974 the

Bureau was put under the Department of the Interior and renamed the Fish and Wildlife Service. For clarity's sake, I refer to the organization throughout the book as the U.S. Fish and Wildlife Service or Fish and Wildlife. (See Chandler, "The U.S. Fish and Wildlife Service"; and Bean, *The Evolution of National Wildlife Law*, pp. 65–66).

Page 30: NASA later added land to the refuge for a total of 126,000 acres: Bensen and Faherty, p. 107.

Page 30: ". . . the operation launch base of today": NASA, *The Kennedy Space Center Story*, p. 16.

Page 30: ". . . shoot ducks in the shadow of a Moon Rocket": Ibid., p. 5.

4 Mosquitoes

Page 32: ". . . It may entirely disappear. . . . ": Letter from Donald Nicholson to Allen J. Duvall, April 30, 1956.

Page 33: ". . . lst Ind MTIPA 7 Aug 61, same subj.": Letter from Colie Houck, Colonel, USAF, to Jack Salmela, August 9, 1961.

Page 34: ". . . be practiced with utmost care.": Provost, *Florida Health Notes*.

Page 34: ". . . to an infinity of natural production": Letter from Provost to Paul Springer, November 22, 1960.

Page 35: "fact yet to be established": Provost, "Impounding Salt Marshes."

Page 35: ". . . sparrow 'refuge' can't be set up . . . across from Titusville": Letter from Maurice Provost to Paul F. Springer, November 22, 1960.

Page 36: echoed some of these sentiments in an earlier letter: Letter from Donald Nicholson to Allen J. Duvall, April 30, 1956.

Page 36: ". . . than he'd ever seen before in one day!": Letter from Maurice Provost to Paul F. Springer, March 21, 1961.

Page 36: impression at secondhand: Jack Salmela had passed this information on to Provost.

Page 37: ducks had always come in prodigious numbers to north Merritt Island: Dwight Cooley, personal communication.

Page 37: ". . . made-to-order for waterfowl management.": Letter from Provost to Paul Springer, March 21, 1961.

Page 38: ". . . so unpredictably a virtual desert": Provost, "Impounding Salt Marshes."

Page 38: "local boy who made good": Charles Trost, personal communication.

Page 38: Salmela was also an avid duck hunter: Joy Mitchell (formerly Salmela), personal communication.

Page 39: Description of airplane accident: Lee Wenner and Jack Salmela, personal communication.

Page 39: went camping together in the St. Johns River valley: Joy Mitchell (formerly Salmela), personal communication.

Page 39: encouraged Bobby to hang around with the graduate student: Jack Salmela, personal communication.

Page 39: learning the broader principles of ecology: Joy Mitchell (formerly Salmela), personal communication.

Page 39: ". . . nature measures it in centuries": Joy Mitchell (formerly Salmela), personal communication.

Page 40: ". . . replaced by freshwater plants": Lon Ellis, personal communication.

Page 40: "ecological rape": Charles Trost, personal communication.

Page 41: ". . . A dusky nest with four young was found during the count": Trost's quarterly report, July 1 to September 30, 1963. Entry for July 17, 1963.

Page 41: "Everyone seemed to agree with this idea": Ibid. Entry for November 16.

Page 41: ". . . for the first time this year": Ibid.

Page 41: strangers to the traditional salt marsh began to take over: Leenhouts and Baker.

Page 42: ". . . mottled nest still had eggs": Trost's quarterly report, July 1 to September 30, 1963. Entry for May 21, 1963.

Page 42: Florida Museum of Natural History: Originally called the Florida State Museum, this later became the Florida Museum of Natural History.

Page 42: Trost captured three more on Merritt Island: They were collected on January 3 (a female); July 28 (a male); and July 30 (a juvenile female). Skins list, Florida Museum of Natural History.

Page 43: ". . . destroyed by the draglines": Ibid. Entry for July 19, 1963.

Page 43: a large alligator: Ibid. Entry for May 14, 1963.

Page 43: ". . . big fish kill in . . . this new impoundment—probably from water loss": Ibid. Entry for May 15, 1963.

Page 43: took up residence in the bushes growing on the dikes: Trost, "Dusky Seaside Sparrow."

Page 43: "With Love": Letter to Lucy Trost from Jack Salmela, June 11, 1969.

Page 44: resistant mosquitoes: Sykes, p. 732.

Page 44: he found only about seventy pairs in four colonies: Ibid., p. 732.

Page 44: ". . . lack of adequate food and cover in extensive impounded areas": Trost, "Study of Wildlife Usage of Salt Marsh."

Page 45: ". . . where their tax dollars have to go": Letter from Maurice W. Provost to Hal Scott, February 7, 1972.

Page 45: "impoundments are definitely changing the present habitat of the dusky seaside sparrow": Letter from Jack Salmela to Curtis Wilson, March 12, 1964.

Page 45: ". . . millions of newly hatched adults without doing something to kill them": Letter from Jack Salmela to Chris Elmore, July 31, 1964.

Page 46: Trost abandoned the field work to enter his Ph.D. program at UCLA: Letter from Allan Cruickshank to Joseph Hickey, November 30, 1967.

Page 46: to take pictures of the countryside: *Florida Today*, "Brevard War Dead at 32," May 17, 1968.

Page 46: the dark granite face of the Vietnam War Memorial in Washington, D.C.: Panel 60 East, Line number 2, May 13, 1968.

Page 47: Arthur Cleveland Bent series on the life histories of North American birds: Trost, "Dusky Seaside Sparrow."

5 If Only

Page 48: ". . . the regret doesn't go away; it grows": Charles Trost, personal communication.

Page 51: Description of great southern white butterflies: Letter from Erik Tetens Nielsen to William R. Opp, December 2, 1984.

6 Endangered

Page 53: *Surveyor 3*: NASA, *The Kennedy Space Center Story*, p. 347.

Page 53: four widely isolated colonies on Merritt Island: Kale, *Ecology and Bioenergetics of the Long-billed Marsh Wren*.

Page 53: The dusky became officially endangered in March: March 11, 1967, 32 FR 4001.

Page 54: the greatest diversity of snail species remaining in the Tennessee-Ohio river system: Davis.

Page 55: for no laws forbade it: Bean, *The Evolution of National Wildlife Law*, p. 21; and Mann and Plummer, "The Butterfly Problem," p. 48.

Page 55: killed . . . the last passenger pigeon in the wild: Day, p. 37. The author does not mention a specific source for this information.

Page 55: in Brevard County at Padget Creek: Fuller, p. 150. Fuller writes:

"Among the last reliable records of wild birds is one of six individuals taken at Padget Creek, Brevard County, Florida on 18 April 1901 and another of thirteen seen at Lake Okeechobee, Florida during April 1904; . . . the last bird collected was very likely a female taken at Orlando on 4 December 1913." Fuller provides no specific sources for this information.

Page 55: ". . . the protection of the government of the United States": Bean, p. 19.

Page 55–56: birds traveling between the two countries: Ibid., p. 20. This law replaced the 1913 law, which advocates feared would be overturned by the U.S. Supreme Count on constitutional grounds. The Migratory Bird Treaty Act was actually signed by Great Britain on behalf of Canada.

Page 56: ". . . no birds for any powers to deal with": Ibid., p. 21.

Page 56: the Migratory Bird Conservation Act of 1929 for federal wildlife refuge acquisition: Ibid., p. 215.

Page 56: the Coordination Act of 1934: Ibid., pp. 180–214. Not to be confused with the Fish and Wildlife Coordination Act of 1976.

Page 56: Bald Eagle Protection Act of 1940: Ibid., pp. 89–99.

Page 56: Endangered Species Preservation Act of 1966: Ibid., p. 319.

Page 56: ". . . its survival requires assistance": Ibid, p. 320.

Page 56: ". . . consistent with their primary purposes": Ibid., p. 322.

Page 57: ". . . must do something about it": From prepared remarks by Herbert Kale at the 1969 conference.

Page 58: he estimated there to be almost nine hundred males: Sharp, "A Population Estimate."

Page 59: Sharp assumed that a female existed for each singing male: Sharp, personal communication. This has been a long-held assumption in the censusing of most songbirds.

Page 59: given half a chance, would survive: Blakey.

Page 59: Curtis Wilson, the refuge manager: Wilson was later promoted to a supervisory position in Atlanta, then to Program Development for Wildlife in Washington, D.C.

Page 60: ". . . [Salmela] more ready to 'yield' on managing for duskies than Curtis!": Letter from Provost to Brian Sharp, January 15, 1969.

Page 60: ". . . some people who just won't be satisfied . . . ": Sharp, entry for personal log, April 23, 1968.

Page 60: "preserve habitat for the majority of the known refuge population of the endangered dusky seaside sparrow . . . ": "Management Proposal for the Dusky Seaside Sparrow Habitat Bureau of Sport Fisheries and Wildlife, Mer-

ritt Island National Wildlife Refuge, Brevard County Florida," approved by
U.S. Fish and Wildlife Service on March 28, 1969.

Page 60: instituting essentially what Charles Trost had called for in his study
five years earlier: Trost, "Study of Wildlife Usage of Salt Marsh," pp. 29-30.

Page 61: research closely resembling that of the 1969 study: The study in
Ecology focused on more than 40 major waterfowl impoundments, flooding
18,476 acres, built by the Michigan Department of Conservation between
1948 and 1959.

Page 61: up to two and a half months of flooding but no more: Brian Sharp,
personal communication.

Page 61: These impoundments were known as Black Point, Marsh Bay, and
Gator Creek: Black Point Impoundment was known technically as T-10-J;
Marsh Bay Impoundment as T-10-K; and Gator Creek Impoundment as T-
24-C.

Page 62: dike at Gator Creek would be breached and remain open year-
round: Management proposal from C. Edward Carlson, regional director of
U.S. Fish and Wildlife Service sent to Jack Salmela, March 28, 1969.

Page 62: an earlier understanding . . . reached back in 1964: "A Memorandum of Understanding between Bureau of Sport Fisheries and Wildlife, Brevard Mosquito Control District, and Florida State Board of Health, January,
1964," states that "The management operation by the Bureau will be conducted in such a manner that it will neither interfere with the District's
mosquito control program, nor create or prolong conditions that favor mosquito production."

Page 62: ". . . cause less harm": Letter from Jack Salmela to C. Edward Carlson,
April 3, 1969.

Page 63: ". . . now ready for your signature": Letter from C. Edward Carlson
to Jack Salmela, April 11, 1969.

Page 63: . . . year-round for mosquito abatement . . . as a "control": Sykes,
pp. 728-729.

Page 63: the dusky for seven months of the year and flooded the other five
for mosquito control: Sykes, p. 729.

Page 63: thirty within the three designated study areas and up to a half dozen
outside them: As shown on Sharp's census map in 1968.

Page 63: Five males lived in the Gator Creek Impoundment several miles to
the south: "Annual Progress Report 1970," Project P-H-6, Regional Office,
Atlanta, p. 2.

Page 63: lived between the study areas: These half dozen are based on Brian
Sharp's survey of 1968.

Page 64: Marsh Bay Impoundment, holding nine duskies, be drained year-round and returned completely to the sparrow: Acreage comes from document of August 1972, "Merritt Island NWR Impoundment Acreage Data," complied by Brevard County Mosquito Control.

Page 64: slim majority, indeed: These figures include the thirty sparrows within the three impoundments, as well as the half-dozen sparrows found outside the study areas by Brian Sharp in 1968. In other words, twenty-one of the thirty-six sparrows on the island, or 58 percent, were given the benefit of management. If only the thirty sparrows within the study areas are included, this is 70 percent. It is not known exactly how many sparrows remained along Gator Creek when the study began.

Page 64: ". . . assure permanent recovery of this remnant population": Letter from C. Edward Carlson to Jack Salmela, March 28, 1969.

Page 64: ". . . This represents a 44 percent reduction in one year": "Annual Progress Report 1970," Project P-H-6, Regional Office, Atlanta.

Page 64: Gator Creek had held five birds in 1969, but only two in 1970: "Report on Dusky Seaside Sparrow" by Endangered Species Biologist, Paul Sykes, January 27, 1971. To regional director, Atlanta.

Page 64: and none after 1971: Sykes, p. 732.

Page 64: but only one the following year . . . their population having fallen by only two: Sykes, "Annual Progress Report 1970."

Page 65: "edge effect": (Minutes of Annual Meeting between the U.S. Fish and Wildlife Service and the Brevard Mosquito Control District, April 6, 1971.) "Edge effect" refers to an area where two habitats overlap. In this case, water holes would have been created. The "edge" where water met the land theoretically would have been an area of increased diversity. In any case, dynamiting would have been of dubious value in creating such an "edge effect," according to Sykes and Sharp (personal communication).

Page 65: "reintroduce individuals onto the refuge from the St. Johns. . . .": "Annual Progress Report 1970," Project P-H-6, Regional Office, Atlanta.

Page 65: Continue the study did, with some modifications: The subdike across Marsh Bay Impoundment was removed.

Page 65: By 1973, only three duskies remained on Merritt Island: James L. Baker, "Progress Report," July 1, 1973; and Sykes, "Decline and Disappearance of Dusky Seaside Sparrow" (see graphs p. 32).

7 The Man on Horseback

Page 66: ". . . and some fear it eventually may be exterminated": Letter from Allan D. Cruickshank to Joseph J. Hickey, November 30, 1967.

Page 67: *Titusville Star-Advocate:* July 5, 1968.

Page 67: his wife's own stay on Merritt Island: Note from Charles Trost to Brian Sharp, April 23, 1968.

Page 68: as well as salt-marsh plants and salt-marsh birds: Sincock.

Page 68: Pedro de Quexas . . . 1519: Douglas, p. 49.

Page 69: ". . . the valley very beautiful to see": Laudonnière.

Page 69–70: Stowe's quote: Stowe, pp. 247–61.

Page 71: christened it *Ammodramus maritimus nigrescens:* Ridgway, *Bulletin: Essex Institute.*

Page 71: insisted that it was a distinct species: Maynard.

Page 72. "The panda is a panda": Schaller, p. 306.

Page 72: about twenty breeding pairs near State Road 50: Nicholson, "Breeding of the Dusky Seaside Sparrow."

Page 72: Howell, Jr. had searched the St. Johns in 1931: Brian Sharp, personal communication.

Page 72: found duskies about seven miles southwest of the Indian River and south of State Road 50: Ibid.

Page 72: ". . . know of these sites!": Notes made by Brian Sharp, June 15, 1968, after visit to Charles E. Carter in Orlando.

Page 73: "Dream Navel orange": letterhead of Royal Purple Citrus Research Nursery stationery, the nursery Donald Nicholson founded in 1930.

Page 73: on his deathbed: Lon Ellis, personal communication. Nicholson's personal collection is now at Clemson University. (Department of Biological Sciences, Clemson University, Clemson, South Carolina.)

Page 74: Trost found five dusky pairs along State Road 50, west of Titusville: Shown on notes and maps sent to Sharp by Trost, April 23, 1968.

Page 75: including a half-dozen singing males a couple of miles southwest of Trost's colony: Sharp, "A Population Estimate of the Dusky Seaside Sparrow."

Page 75: "colony heretofore unknown to the ornithological world": Letter from Brian Sharp to Joseph Hickey, May 13, 1968.

Page 75: ". . . doesn't know he is becoming extinct," Sharp told one reporter: Eberhart, "Rarer Than Whoopers." The wire service copy of the article is subtitled, "Live Only at Cape Kennedy." This article is also among the earliest national printed media reports focusing on the dusky.

Page 76: when it came to endangered species: Eberhart, "The Dwindling Dusky."

Page 76: The "great white bird": Nilsson, p. 167.

Page 76: fame grew with the Apollo launches: Eberhart, "Rarer Than Whoopers." Wire service copy.

Page 76: ". . . cause embarrassment to Mosquito Control": Letter from Brian Sharp to Joseph J. Hickey, May 13, 1968.

Page 76: ". . . woven over the top": Field notes by Brian Sharp, May 14, 1968, "St. Johns Big Colony."

Page 78: ". . . steadiness of the horses": Letter from Brian Sharp to Joseph J. Hickey, May 31, 1968.

Page 79: and about as many females—throughout the St. Johns: Sharp, "A Population Estimate of the Dusky Seaside Sparrow."

Page 79: ". . . any species becoming extinct": *Brevard Sentinel*, March 21, 1969.

Page 79: "Salmela always expressed concern about the dusky": Brian Sharp, personal communication.

Page 80: ". . . credit for initiating this study": Letter from Jack Salmela to Brian Sharp, January 20, 1969.

Page 80: ". . . assistance given Trost by Jack Salmela and the Brevard County Mosquito Control District": Letter from Maurice Provost to Brian Sharp, January 3, 1969. But after looking through the Bent series later on, Provost realized that the Life Histories . . . volumes do not include separate acknowledgments.

Page 80: ". . . part of my soul": Brian Sharp, personal communication.

Page 80: ". . . use of our helicopter . . . ": Handwritten note at bottom of photocopy of "Paradise for Rare Birds," *Star Advocate*, July 8, 1968. Attached to this article is wire copy of Eberhart, "Rarer than Whoopers," April 18, 1968.

Page 81: ". . . extinction on their record": Eberhart, "Rarer than Whoopers." Wire service copy.

Page 81: that the article therefore would not be published: In a handwritten note attached to the wire service copy, Salmela wrote, "The attached article was not published."

Page 81: *Science News*: Eberhart, "The Dwindling Dusky."

Page 81: ". . . live with this sort of thing": Letter from Jack Salmela to Maurice Provost, April 23, 1968.

8 *Road to Nowhere*

Page 82: ". . . the best dusky area": Letter from Joseph Hickey to Alexander Sprunt IV, March 24, 1969.

Page 83: belief seconded by the service's Vero Beach office: Joseph Carroll, personal communication.

Page 83: they would need a road through it: Schenck's comments are contained on page 3 of a memorandum from R. R. Rudolph, assistant regional supervisor, Division of Refuges, to regional supervisor, Division of Refuges, November 16, 1970.

Page 83: and affect water levels: Letter from Brian Sharp to James A. Powell, May 22, 1970.

Page 83: impact of the roadbeds on the marshes: Blakey.

Page 83: ". . . from here to Washington and back": Letter from Herb Kale to William M. Partington, Jr., September 4, 1971.

Page 84: permit for a bridge across the St. Johns: Letter from A. F. Parker, United States Coast Guard, to O. E. Frye, Jr., April 16, 1970.

Page 84: ". . . save a few minutes driving time": Letter from Brian Sharp to James A. Powell, May 22, 1970.

Page 84: ". . . in: order to save a whole species": Letter from Hal Scott to H. A. Solberg, May 17, 1971.

Page 85: presence of I-95 was therefore irrelevant: Herbert Kale, personal communication.

Page 85: ". . . Dante's Inferno": Brian Sharp, personal communication.

Page 85: obliterating five nesting territories: Herbert Kale, personal communication.

Page 88: ". . . be completed prior to the opening of Walt Disney World": *Orlando Sentinel*, March 30, 1971.

9 Cities in the St. Johns

Page 90: $1.5 million bill for completing the systems: "Water worries stunt growth of subdivision," *Florida Today*, July 30, 1984; and Lee Wenner, personal communication.

Page 93: ". . . it's not all that important": Lee Wenner, personal communication.

Page 93: only a dozen pairs remained there: Baker, "Status of the Dusky Seaside Sparrow."

11 Refuge

Page 97: first refuge ever for a songbird: Lynn Greenwalt, personal communication.

Page 98: " . . . Acquisition Review Committee as soon as possible": Memorandum from acting regional supervisor, Division of Refuge, to regional director, September 3, 1969.

Page 99: not a square foot of land had been bought for the dusky: An outline of the complicated process of establishing the refuge is found in a chronology compiled by the Merritt Island National Wildlife Refuge, "History–St. Johns National Wildlife Refuge."

Page 99: outside group: Karl F. Eichhorn, Jr., personal communication.

Page 99: committee to study the problem: Blakey.

Page 100: "Action is urgently needed now": Letter from Karl F. Eichhorn, Jr. to Terry Blunt, May 19, 1970.

Page 100: ". . . on the heads of all of us in Florida": Letter from Herb Kale to Karl F. Eichhorn, Jr., May 22, 1970.

Page 100: ". . . before we can move with our acquisition program": Letter from W. L. Towns to Karl F. Eichhorn, Jr., June 12, 1970.

Page 100: plans to drain the land for development: Letter from Joseph J. Hickey to Allan Cruickshank, February 11, 1970; and *Florida Today*, January 5, 1970.

Page 100-101: forestalling further development in the area: *Conservation Digest*, no. 48, p. 5.

12 Wildfires

Page 102: March 11, 1932: Fuller, pp. 60–61.

Page 102: Department of the Interior: Udall calls for cooperative effort to save wildlife, July 21, 1968.

Page 103: loss of at least twenty birds in the burned areas: Rakestraw, pp. 103-104.

Page 103: leaving fewer duskies each time: Ibid., p. 15.

Page 103: very few escapees could be accounted for: Ibid., p. 15. The explanation of what likely happened to the birds comes from Herb Kale.

Page 104: but not north of State Road 50: Yoder actually made this recommendation after the fires in 1974. Not until the fires the following year was the land actually purchased.

Page 104: when the winter fire hazards would start: Letter from Robert G. Yoder to the regional director, Atlanta, September 11, 1975.

Page 105: No duskies were ever seen there again: Rakestraw, p. 17.

Page 105: less than three dozen males remaining in all of the St. Johns: Baker, "Status of the Dusky Seaside Sparrow." This figure of less than three dozen is a conservative estimate based on the census of 1977, in which twenty-eight males were found in the entire St. Johns.

Page 105: ". . . (over a year and a half or more!)": U.S. Fish and Wildlife Service, *Endangered Species Technical Bulletin.*

Page 105: ". . . (first things first, of course!)": Letter from Herb Kale to Hal Scott, January 16, 1976.

Page 105: "Merritt Island National Wildlife personnel": Letter from Herb Kale to Nathaniel P. Reed, January 20, 1976.

Page 106: ". . . I'll send it on plain stationery": Letter from Herb Kale to Hal Scott, January 16, 1976.

Page 106: ". . . as endangered as is the dusky seaside sparrow": Comparison of Kale's January 15 draft sent to Hal Scott for approval and the January 20 letter actually sent to Nathaniel Reed shows that the "duck hunters" reference was deleted.

Page 106: 28 in the entire St. Johns: Baker, "Status of the Dusky Seaside Sparrow."

Page 106: ". . . commitment to restoration of the dusky": Letter from Lynn Greenwalt to Hal Scott, March 29, 1976.

Page 107: ". . . this fire lane network": Report from St. Johns National Wildlife Refuge, Section I, "General," October 24, 1979.

Page 107: seen since 1977: Report from St. Johns National Wildlife Refuge, October 24, 1979, p. 6. The report reads, "Only 3 colonies of duskies are known to exist; the St. Johns tract colony, the Beeline tract colony and a colony between these two tracts of the St. Johns National Wildlife Refuge. The spring survey indicated there were 9, 11, and 4 males at each colony respectively . . . no females have been seen for the past two years."

13 Collusion

Page 108: ". . . biblical ark afloat": *New York Times,* April 23, 1973.

Page 109: ". . . in furtherance of the purposes of this Act": Bean, pp. 330–31.

Page 109: an endangered species to survive and recover: Bean, p. 333. According to Bean, "As enacted in 1973, the Act neither defined this term nor specified a procedure for its designation."

Page 110: ". . . conditions that favor mosquito production": "Memorandum of Understanding between Bureau of Sport Fisheries and Wildlife, Brevard Mosquito Control District, and Florida State Board of Health for the Administration of Certain Lands Owned by the National Aeronautics and Space Administration, Merritt Island, Florida," January 1964.

Page 111: ". . . if the impoundment is drawn down": Letter from Robert G. Yoder to Jack Salmela, February 5, 1976.

Page 111: had been spotted in the impoundment: Letter from Robert G. Yoder to Jack Salmela, April 27, 1976.

Page 111: Mosquito Control complied: As documented in Salmela's note at bottom on letter from Robert G. Yoder to Jack Salmela, April 27, 1976.

Page 111: "concerning our responsibilities and jurisdiction over mosquito control activities on the refuge": Memorandum from Stephen R. Vehrs to regional director, Fish and Wildlife Service, Atlanta. In this memo Vehrs refers to his August 1978 request. And in a memorandum from David Peterson to regional director, September 27, 1979, Peterson also reports that "it has been over a year since he [Vehrs] requested an opinion from the solicitor's office. . . . "

Page 111: he still had not received a reply: Memorandum from Stephen R. Vehrs to regional director, September 27, 1979: "We still have yet to receive any word about our 11 August 1978 request for a solicitor's opinion. . . . "

Page 111: tougher restrictions for managing the dusky: These were recommended by the Recovery Team and presented to Kenneth Black in a letter by James L. Baker on June 12, 1979.

Page 111–12: at least for part of the year: This so-called Recommendation Four stemmed from the Dusky Seaside Sparrow Recovery Team meeting of June 12, 1979, as contained in a letter from James L. Baker to Kenneth Black on that date.

Page 112: Salmela balked: Memorandum from Stephen R. Vehrs to regional director, September 27, 1979; and Stephen R. Vehrs, personal communication.

Page 112: ". . . implementation is beginning to become difficult": Memorandum from Stephen R. Vehrs to regional director, September 27, 1979.

Page 112: nobody seemed eager to dig into: Stephen R. Vehrs, personal communication.

Page 112: ". . . from authorizing the continuation of such practices": Memorandum to Kenneth Black, regional director, U.S. Fish and Wildlife Service, Atlanta from Raymond C. Coulter, regional solicitor, Southeast Regional Office, April 28, 1980.

Page 113: see if such an exemption had been obtained: Letter to Chuck Hunter, Division of Endangered Species, U.S Fish and Wildlife Service from the author, December 27, 1990.

Page 113: ". . . NASA or the Brevard Mosquito Control District": Letter from Chuck Hunter, Recovery Coordinator, Division of Endangered Species to the author, February 1, 1991.

Page 113: seaside sparrow was spotted for the last time on Merritt Island: Herb Kale, personal communication.

14 Recovery Team

Page 114: ". . . leaders be selected with utmost care": "Endangered and Threatened Species Recovery Plan and Team Guidelines . . . ," U.S. Department of Interior, U.S. Fish and Wildlife Service, Office of Endangered Species, May 20, 1975.

Page 114: Jim Baker, the refuge biologist since 1973: Gail Baker, personal communication.

Page 115: ". . . the same system that ultimately victimized the dusky": Jerome Jackson, personal communication.

Page 116: ". . . to accept Fish and Wildlife's appointment": Lovett Williams, personal communication.

Page 117: ". . . acts of graciousness and, therefore, beauty": Letter from Brian Sharp to Herb Kale, June 7–8, 1969.

Page 118: ". . . we blew it for the dusky": From notes of Norman Boucher, who interviewed Baker on February 27, 1980.

Page 118: From this hybridized union came the U.S. Fish and Wildlife Service: Chandler, pp. 7–8.

Page 118: divvied up into area offices: This history of U.S. Fish and Wildlife Service was drawn from Chandler.

Page 119: ". . . this was partly the reason why": Brian Sharp, personal communication.

Page 119: during the four years Baker headed the recovery team: Letter of July 6, 1982, from regional director of U.S. Fish and Wildlife Service to James L. Baker, stating "Termination of the official status of the team is effective 90 days from the present date."

Page 119: caught twenty-one: Gail Baker, personal communication.

Page 120: two years to review and approve it: Herb Kale, personal communication.

Page 120: . . . and monitor population levels by periodic surveys: "Dusky Seaside Sparrow Recovery Plan," 1979.

Page 121: "doing a fine job": Letter to James L. Baker from regional director July 6, 1982.

Page 121: Only a half dozen remained in the St. Johns: Herb Kale, personal communication.

15 The Decision

Page 122: $2.6 million: Mann and Plummer, 1992, p. 56.

Page 123: ruling overturned: *New York Times*, April 19, 1978.

Page 123: bar opening of the dam: *New York Times*, June 15, 1978.

Page 123-24: Meyner and Simpson quotes: 1978 *Congressional Quarterly Almanac*, p. 78.

Page 124: ". . . the dusky and its final status": Memorandum of September 5, 1978, from Kenneth E. Black to director, U.S. Fish and Wildlife Service, Washington, D.C., and reply of September 27, 1978 from acting associate director, Harold J. O'Connor, to Black. My appreciation to Charles C. Mann for locating these memos.

Page 124: ". . . the most critical time in the existence of this sparrow": Letter from Warren B. King to Lynn Greenwalt, May 17, 1979.

Page 125: would effectively cripple it: Bean, pp. 335-36. Congress reacted to the Reagan administration by passing the Endangered Species Act Amendments of 1982, repealing many of the burdensome requirements imposed earlier.

Page 125: "by digging a few canals": *Sentinel Star*, May 23, 1979.

16 Last Gasp

Page 126: Longstreet's warning: Longstreet.

Page 127: "prevent the immediate extinction of the dusky seaside sparrow": "Program Narrative, Dusky Seaside Sparrow Emergency Program," Florida Game and Fresh Water Fish Commission, 1978.

Page 128: "Seaside sparrows don't 'flock'": Comments on Sharp's copy of "First Draft of the Proposed Dusky Seaside Sparrow Emergency Program," October 6, 1979.

Page 128: he had gone out into the St. Johns marsh: This was on June 6, some months before the emergency meeting. Sharp had been invited down to assess the dusky situation during the breeding season.

Page 128: bleeding water from the refuge: Recommendations from dusky seaside sparrow recovery team meeting of June 5, 6, and 7, as sent to Kenneth Black on June 12, 1979.

Page 128: the ditch had already been plugged: Sharp's belief stated in a letter from Sharp to ARD, Refuges and Wildlife Resources, Portland, Oregon, November 17, 1978.

Page 128: the Hacienda ditch finally was: "Dusky Projects" log of the Merritt

Island National Wildlife Refuge: "Plugging Hacienda Ditch Completed 26 June 1979." During the time of Sharp's visit, the Recovery Team had met and also recommended, officially for the first time, that the Hacienda ditch (the north-south ditch alongside Hacienda Road) be "immediately plugged..."

Page 128: "Why has this canal not been plugged?": Letter from Warren B. King to Lynn Greenwalt, May 17, 1979.

Page 129: The commissioners . . . ran Brevard County: Herb Kale, personal communication.

Page 130: ". . . too late with too little": Memorandum from C. H. Trost, Trip Report to Titusville, Florida, June 5-6, 1979.

Page 130: ". . . to continue in its natural habitat": Letter from Florida Game and Fresh Water Fish Commission to Brian Sharp, March 6, 1979.

Page 130: dusky was already doomed in the wild: "Notes on the meeting of seaside sparrow biologists to advise the Game and Fresh Water Fish Commission at Gainesville, Florida, 17-18 February 1979."

17 The Last Wild Dusky

Page 131-134: Capture of Aluminum Green described by Bill Leenhouts, personal communication.

Page 131: housing developments through his habitat: *Bird Conservation*, 1983, p. 129.

Page 132: number 1011-41278: Herb Kale, personal communication.

Page 132: just south of State Road 50: Bill Leenhouts, personal communication.

Page 132: a permit to capture the survivors: Endangered Species Permit PRT 2-4329, issued on July 11, 1980.

Page 133: from the west coast of Florida: Summary of Activities under USFWS Permit PRT 2-4329 (unpublished).

Page 133: had refused to buy a few years earlier: Herb Kale, personal communication.

Page 134: ". . . to regret our aesthetic destitution later": Sharp, "Let's Save the Dusky Seaside Sparrow," p. D-11.

Page 134: Allan Cruickshank died on October 11, 1974: Helen Cruickshank, personal communication.

Page 135: burned beyond recognition: Dorn Whitmore, personal communication.

18 To Recreate a Sparrow

Page 138: first known breeding of any type of seaside sparrow in captivity: Post and Antonio.

Page 139: "happy accident": William Post, personal communication.

Page 139: none of the duskies was eaten: Post and Antonio, "Breeding and Rearing of Seaside Sparrows"; and Webber and Post, "Breeding Seaside Sparrows in Captivity."

Page 140: ". . . all we want is an okay": Letter from Thomas E. Lovejoy to Ron Lambertson, May 5, 1981.

Page 140: ". . . alternative [than breeding them]": Letter from Warren B. King to editor, *New York Times*, January 27, 1981.

Page 140: ". . . but come to terms with them we must": Letter from Jon M. Jensen to William Post, May 5, 1981.

Page 141: ". . . Ineffective as a means of preserving a taxon": Letter from Colonel Robert M. Brantly to Kenneth Black, June 24, 1980.

Page 141: ". . . hybridization of the dusky seaside sparrow": Letter from Kenneth Black to Colonel Robert M. Brantly, Florida Game and Fresh Water Fish Commission, July 11, 1980.

Page 141: ". . . we were throwing good money after bad": Kenneth Black, personal communication.

Page 142: ". . . Economic necessity, logic, and hard decision are something else": Charles Hillinger, *Los Angeles Times*, October 19, 1980.

Page 142: ". . . maximize your minimum losses": Bill Leenhouts, personal communication.

Page 142: ". . . that's what it was": Bill Leenhouts, personal communication.

Page 143: ". . . It would take a lot of guts to avow triage publicly": Kenneth Black, personal communication.

Page 143: ". . . they will allow them to die in captivity": Letter from Herb Kale to a Mr. Morton, National Zoological Park, October 13, 1980.

Page 143: viable dusky seaside sparrow population: Resolution passed by Florida Audubon Society and sent by Peter Rhodes Mott to Lynn A. Greenwalt on September 22, 1980.

Page 144: Endangered Species Act of 1973, as amended: The amendment defined a subspecies as "any species or subspecies of fish or wildlife or plant and any distinct population segment of any species of vertebrate fish or wildlife which interbreeds when mature" (see James).

Page 144: ". . . involved in a crossbreeding project": Letter from Harold O'Connor to Peter Rhodes Mott, October 29, 1980.

Page 144: ". . . We hybridized Peregrines and no one squawked": Fish and Wildlife Service Inter-Office Transmittal, September 8, 1980, from Kenneth M. Chitwood to manager, Merritt Island National Wildlife Refuge.

Page 144: moved to . . . Santa Fe Community College in Gainesville: "Dusky Seaside Sparrow Weights" from "Notes on Captive Maintenance of Seaside Sparrows Genus: *Ammospiza* at Santa Fe Community College Teaching Zoo" by James Brack Barker, September 1981. (The actual transfer of the birds took place in April 1981, in two different groups.) And letter from David W. Peterson, assistant area manager of Fish and Wildlife, to Herb Kale, October 14, 1980.

Page 144: $40,000: "Cooperative Agreement Between the U.S. Fish and Wildlife Service Department of the Interior and the Santa Fe Community College." Advance copy of agreement.

Page 144: ". . . You should get a nice profit on it": Joanne Fanizza, "Endangered Dusky Seaside Sparrow Gets Home at SFCC," *Gainesville Sun*, October 17, 1980.

Page 145: ". . . they took away the birds": William Post, personal communication.

Page 145: advocates of crossbreeding: Jim Ellis, personal communication.

Page 146: die in their natural habitat: *New York Times*, January 19, 1981. The article attributes quote to David W. Petersen, assistant area manager for the Fish and Wildlife Service.

Page 146: ". . . It was a dangerous time": Jim Ellis, personal communication.

Page 146: "a lead balloon": Letter from Herb Kale to Simon Lyster, Defenders of Wildlife, December 30, 1980.

Page 147: stored at Fish and Wildlife's Patuxent Wildlife Research Center: Letter from F. Eugene Hester to John William Hardy, May 15, 1981.

Page 147: ". . . destruction of the habitat itself": Letter from S. Dillon Ripley to John Spinks, May 6, 1981.

Page 148: ". . . to fall back on seems to me to be simply irresponsible": Letter from John William Hardy to F. Eugene Hester, May 21, 1981.

Page 149: ". . . deranged criminal determined to commit suicide": Webber and Post.

Page 150: ". . . a biological process that goes on all the time in nature": James, "Miscegenation in the Dusky Seaside Sparrow?"; and O'Brien and Mayr, "Bureaucratic Mischief."

Page 150: ". . . are not covered by the act": Memorandum from Ronald E. Lambertson, assistant solicitor to chief, Division of Law Enforcement, U.S. Fish and Wildlife Service, May 18, 1977.

Page 151: ". . . will be greatly frustrated if hybrids of such species are not covered by the act": Ibid.

Page 151: ". . . opinion reconsidered as soon as possible": Memorandum from Harold O'Connor to solicitor's office, July 21, 1977.

Page 152: ". . . make that language at least latently ambiguous": Memorandum from acting assistant solicitor Donald J. Barry to Harold O'Connor, August 2, 1977.

Page 152: ". . . obituary for the population": Letter from Herb Kale to Simon Lyster, December 30, 1980.

19 Bureaucracy

Page 153: ". . . 50-50 mix of dusky and Scott's": Letter from David W. Peterson to Ms. H. L. Keenan, September 8, 1981.

Page 154: "Copies to *everybody*": Letter from John William Hardy to David W. Peterson, September 24, 1981.

Page 154: permission would have to be granted by November 1: Letter from John W. Hardy to director of U.S. Fish and Wildlife Service, September 2, 1981.

Page 155: ". . . horror story out of Washington": Letter from Herb Kale to F. Eugene Hester, October 30, 1981.

Page 155: ". . . regardless of the outcome": Letter from Herb Kale to F. Eugene Hester, October 20, 1981.

Page 156: ". . . as transitory perhaps as a house of cards": Letter from S. Dillon Ripley to James G. Watt, August 4, 1981.

Page 157: ". . . males will still be alive at that time [next year]": Letter from S. Dillon Ripley to John Spinks, May 6, 1981.

Page 157: ". . . I hope it is published soon": Letter from Herb Kale to Eugene S. Morton, October 13, 1980.

Page 157: ". . . racism or miscegenation": James.

Page 158: ". . . I hope that will include your superiors": Letter from John W. Hardy to director of U.S. Fish and Wildlife Service, November 4, 1981.

Page 158: ". . . a breeding project for the 1983 breeding season": Memorandum sent out September 24 (year not given) by Herb Kale. From references in it, this memo must have been written in 1982 (e.g., Ellis's loaning blueprints of cages to Cook).

Page 159: ". . . offspring on any national wildlife refuge": Letter from Robert E. Putz, acting director, U.S. Fish and Wildlife Service, to Peter R. Mott, September 13, 1982.

20 Magic Kingdom

Page 160: since their capture on the St. Johns two years earlier: Charlie Cook, personal communication.

Page 163: tumor had invaded Red's abdomen and chest cavity: Final Necropsy Report, N83-941, Red Band, September 10, 1983, Veterinary Medical Teaching Hospital, University of Florida.

Page 163: ". . . taxidermist for the job": Letter from Steve Vehrs to Don Wood, March 6, 1985.

Page 165: each bird was fed ten crickets and five mealworms: Kale, *Florida Field Naturalist*.

21 Final Rest

Page 166: last duskies had come to Discovery Island: Letter from Walter O. Stieglitz, acting regional director of U.S. Fish and Wildlife Service to Peter R. Mott, January 28, 1983.

Page 167: ". . . conservation community and by the public in general": Letter from Peter R. Mott to Richard Nunis, February 8, 1983.

Page 167: ". . . billed as a fantasy land where dreams almost always come true": *Miami Herald*, September 10, 1984.

Page 167: an unexpected phone call from the service: Jim Ellis, personal communication.

Page 167: "I'm tempted to say, Eureka!": Victoria Churchville, *Orlando Sentinel*, August 25, 1983.

Page 167: ". . . you'll always have a hybrid, not a dusky": Ibid.

Page 168: ". . . faulty biological opinion": Letter from Herb Kale to Jim Ellis, September 2, 1983.

Page 169: ". . . I can offer you our ideas": Letter from Jim Ellis to Herb Kale, September 8, 1982.

Page 169: ". . . lost the birds long before we have the chance to breed them": Letter from Herb Kale to Jim Ellis, September 23, 1982.

Page 170: the whim of commercial as well as biological considerations: Herb Kale, personal communication.

Page 170: ". . . I wanted nothing further to do with the project": Jim Ellis, personal communication.

Page 170: *Ammospiza*: At the time, this was the accepted genus name.

Page 170: Fish and Wildlife rejected both ideas: Jim Ellis, personal communication.

Page 170: ". . . we hope the dusky will live forever": Victoria Churchville, "Tiny Baby Bird Raises Hope for 'Duskies,'" *Orlando Sentinel*, August 25, 1983.

Page 171: ". . . who make the financial decisions for this project": Letter from Herb Kale to Charlie Cook, June 9, 1983.

Page 171: "turn a cat loose on the remaining birds": Charlie Cook, personal communication.

Page 171: Blue . . . died of kidney failure: Herb Kale, personal communication.

Page 172: ". . . who otherwise would have never cared": Letter from Charlie Cook to Herb Kale (undated).

Page 173: breaking its neck: Herb Kale, personal communication.

Page 173: Orange was nearly twelve years old: There were no published detailed accounts of the history of the duskies at Discovery Island. Most of the details of the history given here were provided by Kale and Cook. See also Kale, "Duskies Transferred to Discovery Island"; Kale and Cook, "Dusky Seaside Sparrow Update," 1984, 1985.

22 A Special Kind of Deprivation

Page 177: ". . . to pay the sum of $500.00": Letter from "A. Davenport Critchley" to Martin Joel, May 26, 1977.

Page 177: law enforcement division of the U.S. Fish and Wildlife Service: Letter from Herb Kale to Allen Morgan, June 22, 1977.

Page 177: ". . . laws were violated by the use of official stationery": Letter from James Baird to Herb Kale, June 28, 1977.

23 Eternal Moment

Page 180: ". . . slower and less sure in his landings": Steinhart, 1986.

Page 181–82: The account of Orange's death was provided by Lisa Danforth in a personal interview at Discovery Island on June 26, 1990.

Page 182: "He's gone, Herb. Orange is dead": Charlie Cook, personal communication.

Page 183: ". . . Now, then, let us depart in peace": Brian Sharp, July 1, 1987.

Page 183: ". . . or hear that song in the St. Johns marshes": Letter from Herb Kale to Brian Sharp, July 16, 1987.

Page 183: ". . . nor you either": Letter from Kathi to Brian Sharp (undated).

24 Broken Images

Page 184: an encouraging word: Joy Mitchell (formerly Salmela), personal communication.

Page 185: ". . . surveys of refuge lands": "Citation for Conservation Service," The secretary of the interior, 1986.

Page 186: ". . . except to show them where they were": Letter from Jack Salmela to Joseph K. Shisler, May 6, 1981.

Epilogue

Page 193: geneticists at the University of Georgia: Avise and Nelson.

Page 194: "a devastating event": Lisanne Renner, "Last Link to Dusky Blows Away at Disney," *Orlando Sentinel*, June 16, 1989.

Page 194: In a detailed letter: Letter from Herbert W. Kale to author, June 14, 1992.

Page 194: telltale signs of rat predation: Ibid.

Page 195: ". . . what else can we do but accept [the statements] in good faith": Ibid.

Page 195: Keven Myers told me: interview with Keven Myers, general manager of Fort Wilderness, June 25, 1990.

Page 196: National Climactic Data Center: Telephone interview, Alex Graumann, August 15, 1990.

Page 196: I then ordered weather-radar records: SRRS Product Retrieval Narrative Radar Summaries, March 17–28, 1989, National Climactic Data Center, Asheville, NC.

Page 197: if I could see the logs: Interview with Bill Gillett and Keven Myers, Discovery Island, June 25, 1990.

Page 197: ". . . erroneous information about the records": Letter from Lt. John L. Moran, wildlife inspector, Florida Game and Fresh Water Fish Commission, to the author, August 9, 1990.

Page 197: ". . . logbooks are not available": Letter from Bob Penn, director of Environmental Affairs, to the author, September 7, 1990.

Page 197: "They must be in a deep vault somewhere": Telephone conversation, Bill Gillett, October 16, 1991.

Page 198: Postscript: December 12, 1990; 55FR 51112-14

Bibliography

American Ornithologists' Union. *Checklist of North American Birds*. 5th ed. Baltimore: American Ornithologists' Union, 1975, 595–97.

————. *Thirty-fourth Supplement to the American Ornithologists' Union Checklist of North American Birds*. Supplement to *Auk* 99(1982):1–16CC.

————. *Thirty-second Supplement to the American Ornithologists' Union Checklist of North American Birds*. Supplement to *Auk* 90(1973):411–19.

Antonio, Frederick B., and Ellis, J. "History and Current Status of the Dusky Seaside Sparrow." American Association of Zoological Parks and Aquariums Regional Conference Proceedings, 1981, 57–66.

Ashton, Ray E., Jr., and Ashton, Patricia Sawyer. *Handbook of Reptiles and Amphibians of Florida: Part 1, Snakes*. Miami: Windward Inc., 1981.

Audubon, John J. "The Sea-side Finch." *Ornithological Biography* 1(1831): 470–71.

Avise, John C., and Nelson, William S. "Molecular Genetic Relationships of the Extinct Dusky Seaside Sparrow." *Science* 243(3 February 1989):646–48.

Baker, James L. "Preliminary Studies of the Dusky Seaside Sparrow on the St. John's National Wildlife Refuge." Proceedings of Annual Conference

Southeastern Association of Game and Fish Commissioners 27(1973): 207–14.

———. "Status of the Dusky Seaside Sparrow." *Georgia Department of Natural Resources Technical Bulletin*, 1978, 94–99.

Baker, James L.; Kale, Herbert W. II; and Williams, L. E. "Dusky Seaside Sparrow Recovery Plan." Dusky Seaside Sparrow Recovery Team, U.S. Fish and Wildlife Service, 1979.

Baynard, Oscar E. "The Dusky Seaside Sparrow." *Oologist* 31(1914):130–34.

Bean, Michael J. *The Evolution of National Wildlife Law.* Revised and expanded edition. New York: Praeger, 1983.

Bensen, Charles D., and Faherty, William Barnaby. *Moonport: A History of Apollo Launch Facilities and Operation.* The NASA History Series. John F. Kennedy Space Center: NASA, 1978.

Blakey, Millard L. "Resumé of the Dusky Seaside Sparrow Conference." Recorded by Conference Coordinator, 1969. Unpublished.

Bureau of Entomology. *Handbook of Mosquito Control for Florida.* Department of Health and Rehabilitative Services, Division of Health, 1974.

Cabell, Branch, and Hanna, A. J. *The St. Johns: A Parade of Diversities.* New York: Farrar & Rinehart, Inc., 1943.

Chandler, William J. "The U.S. Fish and Wildlife Service." *Audubon Wildlife Report* (1985):1–24.

Chapman, Frank M. *Handbook of Birds of Eastern North America.* New York: D. Appleton and Co., 1977.

Davis, George M. "Rare and Endangered Species: A Dilemma." *Frontiers* 41(1977):12–14.

Day, David. *The Doomsday Book of Animals.* New York: Viking, 1981.

DeLorme Mapping Company. *Florida Atlas.* Freeport, Maine, 1987.

Douglas, Marjory Stoneman. *Florida: The Long Frontier.* New York: Harper and Row, 1967.

Eberhart, Jonathan. "The Dwindling Dusky." *Science News* 93(25 May 1968): 501–2.

Bibliography

Eberhart, Jonathan. "Rarer Than Whoopers." *Science News* (18 April 1968).

Ehrenhard, J. W. "Canaveral National Seashore: Assessment of Archaeological and Historical Resources," 1976. Unpublished.

Federal Writers' Project. *Florida: A Guide to the Southernmost State.* American Guide Services. New York: Oxford University Press, 1944.

Fleming, Glenn; Genelle, Pierre; and Long, Robert W. *Wild Flowers of Florida.* Miami: Banyan Books, 1984.

Florida Game and Fresh Water Fish Commission. *A Checklist of Florida's Amphibians and Reptiles.* Tallahassee: Florida Game and Fresh Water Fish Commission, 1990.

————. *A Checklist of Florida's Birds.* Tallahassee: Florida Game and Fresh Water Fish Commission, 1984.

————. *A Checklist of Florida's Mammals.* Tallahassee: Florida Game and Fresh Water Fish Commission, 1987.

Fuller, Errol. *Extinct Birds.* New York: Facts on File, 1987.

Gill, Joan E., and Read, Beth R., eds. *Born of the Sun: The Official Florida Bicentennial Book.* Hollywood: Florida Bicentennial Commemorative Journal, 1975.

Griffin, John W., and Miller, James J. "Cultural Resource Reconnaissance of Merritt Island National Wildlife Refuge," 1978. Unpublished.

Gillett, J. D. *The Mosquito: Its Life, Activities, and Impact on Human Affairs* New York: Doubleday, 1972.

Howell, A. H. *Florida Bird Life.* New York: Coward-McCann, Inc., 1932.

James, Frances C. "Miscegenation in the Dusky Seaside Sparrow?" *BioScience* 30 (December 1980):800–801.

Kadlec, J. A. "Effects of a Drawdown on a Waterfowl Impoundment." *Ecology* 43(1962):267–81.

Kale, Herbert W. II. "Dusky Seaside Sparrow—Gone Forever?" *Florida Naturalist* 54(1981):3–4.

————. "Duskies Transferred to Discovery Island." *Florida Naturalist* 57(1983).

227

————. *Ecology and Bioenergetics of the Long-billed Marsh Wren*, Telmatodytes palustris griseus (*Brewster*) *in Georgia Salt Marshes*. Cambridge, MA: Nuttall Ornithology Club No. 5, 1965.

————. "Endangered Species: Dusky Seaside Sparrow." *Florida Naturalist* 50(1977):16–21.

————. "The 1980 Dusky Seaside Sparrow Survey." *Florida Field Naturalist* 9(1981):64–67.

————. "A Status Report on the Dusky Seaside Sparrow." *Bird Conservation* 1(1983): 129.

————. "The Uniqueness of the Dusky." *Florida Naturalist* 62(1989):15.

Kale, Herbert W. II, and Cook, Charlie. "Dusky Seaside Sparrow Update." *Florida Naturalist* 56(1984):3.

————. "Dusky Seaside Sparrow Update." *Florida Naturalist* 58(1985).

Laudonnière, René Goulaine de. *Three Voyages*. Translated by Charles E. Bennett. Gainesville: University of Florida Press, 1974.

Leenhouts, Willard P., and Baker, James L. "Vegetation Dynamics in Dusky Seaside Sparrow Habitat on Merritt Island National Wildlife Refuge." *Wildlife Society Bulletin* 10(1982).

Levey, Richard S.; Barton, David; and Riorda, Timothy B. "An Archaeological Survey of Cape Canaveral Air Force Station." Resource Analysts, Inc., Bloomington, IN. Prepared for National Park Service, Southeast Regional Office, Archeological Services Branch, Atlanta, GA, 1984. Unpublished.

Lewis, Richard S. *Appointment on the Moon*. New York: Ballantine Books, Inc., 1969.

Long, G. A. "Antiquities Resources." John F. Kennedy Space Center: NASA, 1969. Unpublished.

Longstreet, Rubert J. "Dusky Seaside Colony Endangered." *Florida Naturalist* 26(1955):78.

MacKinnon, Douglas, and Baldanza, Joseph. *Footprints: The 12 Men Who Walked on the Moon Reflect on Their Flights, Their Lives and the Future*. Washington, D.C.: Acropolis Books, Ltd., 1989.

Bibliography

Mann, Charles C., and Plummer, Mark L. "The Butterfly Problem." *Atlantic*, January 1992.

Martinez, C. A. "Cultural Resource Assessment—(Merritt Island/Cape Canaveral Area)," 1977. Unpublished.

Maynard, Charles J. "A New Species of Finch from Florida." *American Sportsman* 5(16 January 1875):248.

NASA. *The Kennedy Space Center Story*. John F. Kennedy Space Center: Public Affairs Office, undated.

—————. *Spaceport News*, 8 August 1963, 4.

Nilsson, Greta. *Endangered Species Handbook*. Washington, D.C.: Animal Welfare Institute, 1983.

Nicholson, Donald J. "Breeding of the Dusky Seaside Sparrow on the Mainland of Florida." *Auk* 46(1969).391.

—————. "Nesting Habits of Seaside Sparrows in Florida." *Wilson Bulletin* 40(1928):225-37.

O'Brien, Stephen H., and Mayr, Ernst. "Bureaucratic Mischief." *Science* 251 (1991):1187-88.

Post, William, and Antonio, Frederick B. "Breeding and Rearing of Seaside Sparrows (*Ammospiza martima*) in Captivity." *International Zoo Yearbook* 12(1981):123-28.

Post, William. "The Influence of Rice Rats *Oryzomys palustris* on the Habitat Use of the Seaside Sparrow *Ammospiza maritima*." *Behavioral Ecology and Sociobiology* 9(1981):35-40.

Provost, Maurice W. "Impounding Salt Marshes for Mosquito Control . . . and Its Effects on Bird Life." *Florida Naturalist* 32(1959).

—————. Title of article unavailable. *Florida Health Notes* 40 (May 1948):103.

Quay, Thomas L. et al., eds. "The Seaside Sparrow, Its Biology and Management." Occasional Papers of the North Carolina Biological Survey, 1983-1985.

Rakestraw, James Louis. "Changes in Number, Distribution, and Behavior of the Dusky Seaside Sparrow Following Winter Wildfire." Master's thesis, University of Georgia, 1977.

Rambler. *Guide to Florida.* Reprint. 1975. Full citation unavailable.

Raven, Peter H. and Johnson, George B. *Biology.* St. Louis: Times Mirror/ Mosby College Publishing, 1986.

Ridgway, Robert. "On Some New Forms of American Birds." *Bulletin: Essex Institute* 5(1873):198.

————. *A Manual of North American Birds.* Philadelphia: J. B. Lippincott Co, 1887.

Robbins, Chandler S.; Bruun, Bertel; and Zim, Herbert S. *Birds of North America.* New York: Golden Press, 1983.

Schaller, George B. "Secrets of the Wild Panda." *National Geographic*, March 1986.

Sharp, Brian E. "Conservation of the Dusky Seaside Sparrow on Merritt Island, Florida." *Biological Conservation* 1(1969):175–76.

————. "Let's Save the Dusky Seaside Sparrow." *Florida Naturalist* 42 (1969):68–70.

————. "Numbers, Distribution, and Management of the Dusky Seaside Sparrow." Master's thesis, University of Wisconsin, 1968.

————. "A Population Estimate of the Dusky Seaside Sparrow." *The Wilson Bulletin* 82(1970):158–66.

Sincock, John L. "Waterfowl Ecology in the St. Johns River Valley." Federal Aic Project W-19-R. Florida Game and Fresh Water Fish Commission, 10 May 1958.

Sprunt, Alexander S., Jr. *Florida Bird Life.* New York: Coward-McCann, Inc., 1954, 473–481.

Steinhart, Peter. "Synthetic Species." *Audubon* 188(September 1986):8–11.

Stowe, Harriet Beecher. *Palmetto-Leaves.* Gainesville: University of Florida Press, 1968.

Sykes, Paul W., Jr. "Decline and Disappearance of the Dusky Seaside sparrow from Merritt Island, Florida." *American Birds* 34(September 1980): 728–37.

Taylor, D. Scott. "The Ubiquitous Mosquito." *Florida Naturalist* (Winter 1988):8–11.

Teal, John, and Teal, Mildred. *Life and Death of the Salt Marsh*. New York: Audubon/Ballantine, 1972.

Trost, Charles H. "Dusky Seaside Sparrow." In *Life Histories of North American Cardinals, Grosbeaks, Buntings, Towhees, Finches, Sparrows, and Allies* by A. C. Bent, edited by O. L. Austin, Jr. *U.S. Natural Museum Bulletin* 237: 849–59.

————. "Study of Wildlife Usage of Salt Marsh on East Coast of Florida Before and After Impoundment for Mosquito and Sandfly Control." U.S. Department of the Interior, Fish and Wildlife Service. (Contract: 14-16-0008-623.) Unpublished.

U.S. Fish and Wildlife Service. "Determination of Critical Habitat for Six Endangered Species." *Federal Register* 42(11 August 1977):40, 685–40, 691.

————. "The Dusky Seaside Sparrow." Biological Services Program, FWS/OBS-80/01, March 1980.

————. "Endangered and Threatened Species Recovery Plan and Team Guidelines . . ." Office of Endangered Species, 20 May 1975.

————. *Endangered Species Technical Bulletin* 2, reprint, October 1985, 1.

————. *Fish and Wildlife News*, September–October 1986, 5.

————. "Special Report: Future of Dusky May Depend on Captive Propagation." *Endangered Species Technical Bulletin*, April 1980.

Webber, Thomas A., and Post, William. "Breeding Seaside Sparrows in Captivity." In *The Seaside Sparrow: Its Biology and Management* edited by Thomas L. Quay et al. Occasional Papers of the North Carolina Biological Survey, October 1983–85.

Wilford, John Noble. *We Reach the Moon*. New York: Bantam Books, 1969.

Index

Index